THE
STATESMANSHIP OF JESUS

A Study in the Wonderful Epistle to the Hebrews

By

Rev. Wm. Pascoe Goard
LL.D., F.R.G.S., F.R.E.S.

A REPRINT OF 1929 EDITION BY
COVENANT PUBLISHING COMPANY, BRITAIN

PUBLISHED BY
ARTISAN SALES
P.O. BOX 1497 • THOUSAND OAKS
CALIF. 91360 U.S.A.

ISBN: 0-934666-35-0
LIBRARY OF CONGRESS CATALOG CARD NUMBER: 89-83501

1

THE
STATESMANSHIP OF JESUS

CONTENTS

FOREWORD

By THE REV. JAMES MOUNTAIN, D.D.

IT is a real pleasure to me to accede to the request of the able Author that I would write a Foreword to this book.

While perusing the proofs, I have felt myself illuminated, instructed and cheered ; and I am quite sure that my experience will be repeated in that of thousands into whose hands this volume may come.

The first thing which impresses me is the *doctrinal soundness* of the book. The Rev. William Pascoe Goard believes the Bible from cover to cover, and his knowledge of it is very extensive. He contends also that men should have a definite doctrinal faith—Evangelical and Biblical.

In these days of loose thinking his book will have an important mission in this respect.

Another thing which impresses me is the *originality* of the book. There is no striving after sensational effect. The " old paths " are carefully observed, and yet one feels that one is not reading platitudes, but original ideas from the fully inspired and ever-living Word ; or else that he is viewing old ideas expressed with originality and sparkling with a new lustre. Mr. Pascoe Goard deals largely in short sentences, which sometimes are apophthegms, but which require careful thought before their truth and beauty are fully perceived.

But there is yet a third point which delights me in this volume, namely : *the discovery of the House of Israel* (Ephraim Israel) where superficial readers would not perceive them.

In Mr. Goard's hands the Epistle to the Hebrews gives forth its complete message—the Faithfulness of Jehovah, the Redemption of Israel, and the Atoning Sacrifice for the sin of the world.

May God's richest blessing rest upon this book ; upon its gifted Author ; and upon *The National Message and Banner,* whose Editorial Chair he so worthily occupies!

JAMES MOUNTAIN

St. John's Manse,
    Tunbridge Wells.

INTRODUCTION

THE Epistle to the Hebrews stands forth as unique among the Epistles.

The first question to strike the reader of the Epistle is that of *authorship*. The other Epistles are signed, or indication is given as to the authorship. But no human signature is attached to this great Epistle.

Much questioning has been heard as to authorship, and much comment as to why no name has been signed to its wonderful pages.

Yet, it seems to us, the Epistle is signed; and with a Name which is bound to command the utmost veneration and reverence.

In the days which saw the production of the New Testament Epistles, it was the custom *to sign* the letter first, and then to follow the signature with the matter to be dealt with. Thus "Paul a servant of Jesus Christ," and so on in the other Epistles. The first word was the signature of the author.

We look to the first word of the Epistle to the Hebrews for the signature of the author. So strange is the Name in that place, that we turn away from it with the impression that the Epistle commences with the introduction of matter to be dealt with, without any signature at all. But such is not the case.

The first word of the Epistle is " GOD." But as we follow the theme immediately introduced, we find that GOD is not the theme of the Epistle. Halting in our thought ; considering the relationship of that first Name to the remainder of the Epistle, we are startled with the conviction that " GOD " *stands to that Epistle as the signature of the author of the Epistle.*

It is little wonder that men have failed to grasp the significance of the Name so placed, and that they have turned away saying " GOD " is the theme of the Epistle, and the author who develops the theme is unknown.

Instead of that we shall assume that " God " is the signature of Him who through human agency indeed, *presents and develops the theme of the Epistle.*

If this be the true relationship of the Name to the Epistle : then we are about to read a literary production of unusual sacredness in character and authority even in Bible literature. Then we are about to read a letter from Our Father, who is " the Father of Our Lord Jesus Christ."

In the Old Testament we find many documents signed with the Divine name " I AM, JEHOVAH." Of the New Testament, this Epistle alone bears, in the signature place, the Name " GOD." " The Revelation of Jesus Christ, which God gave unto Him " bears the name of Jesus Christ, the "Alpha and Omega," " the first and the last." The remainder of the books of the New Testament bear the names of Evangelists and Apostles.

INTRODUCTION

Thus, among the books of the New Testament this Epistle would rank first, in view of the signature name " GOD."

What is there in the nature and message of the Epistle which should call for such a startling divergence from the lines of ordinary inspiration, in which lines " Holy men of God wrote and spoke as they were moved by the Holy Ghost " ?

This question is answered by the nature of the theme.

The theme of the Epistle, immediately introduced, and followed with Divine Majesty from paragraph to paragraph is :

GOD, the Son.

Thus it is introduced to us.

" GOD, who at sundry times and in divers manners spake in time past unto the fathers by the prophets, hath in these last days spoken unto us by His Son ; Whom . . . :"

Now follows a presentation of the Son, a declaration of His Person ; biological order of life ; essential Deity ; of His Divine activity as the Maker of the earth and the heavens ; the Upholder of all things ; the Remover of the heavens and the earth ; of His Saviourship ; and of His Majesty.

Then a declaration by the Father, " God," of *the essential Deity of the Son.*

Then a comparison of the angels with the Son, showing that they are in all things inferior to Him.

Again, there is the declaration of His becoming

9

incarnate, and of His taking upon Himself "the seed of Abraham."

Thus the great Message speeds forward, traversing a field of fact and truth much of which is above and beyond the experience of men, and the knowledge of the schools of men.

As we read and ponder all these things we see why God should have taken this phase of Divine Revelation into His own hands, and why this most marvellous Epistle should be signed by the name " GOD."

The vividness, and the matter presented in this Epistle, marks it out as distinct from all the other Epistles.

The theme is exalted above that of the writings of St. John ; breathing the very spirit of *the majesty of God*. While the writings of St. John breathe the very *spirituality* of God. Perhaps the terms we have used, " the Spirit of God " and " the Spirituality of God " will illustrate what we desire to convey.

High ; Holy ; Breathing the very Spirit, God, as this Epistle does, *its revelation is concerned with the very facts and organisations of men on earth.*

It begins with the elements and compounds of which the earth is composed, before there was a conscious mind on earth to respond to Spirituality. It deals with particles of matter, with gases, vapours, liquids, grains of sand, particles of mud, with rocks, and soil, with land and sea, in the making of the earth and the heavens.

For ages and ages this was the field of the

INTRODUCTION

activity of the Maker of the earth and the heavens.

It deals with Angel hosts, and their activities ; "[sent forth."

It deals with " the seed of Abraham," selected among the families of the earth to be the administrative agency of the Lord among men.

It deals with the Covenants, national and racial, which God made with Abraham, Isaac and Jacob.

It deals with the original Kingship which existed before Abraham was ; which came into contact with Abraham ; and received in the person of Melchisedec the homage and tithes of Abraham, and which blessed him.

It deals with the seat of that Kingship in the earth ; " Salem."

It shows that Kingship was ordained to be the Kingship of Jesus Christ ; God the Son.

It shows that that Kingship shall be in the seed of Abraham through Isaac, that its capital shall be Jerusalem, and that it shall be a Kingdom without end.

Thus the theme of this Epistle is racial, national, world-wide.

The common things ; the ordinary things ; the national things ; are made to breathe the very Spirit of God. Governments, Kings, marching armies, administrative courts, national administration are made to stand out as the field of the administration of God the Son Who is :

" King of Righteousness,"
" King of Salem,"

" King of Peace."

It is clear that we are traversing a field of vision and of fact that is higher than the wisdom of men. God alone could testify to all these infinitely exalted things. No other book, nor Epistle of the Bible traverses more exalted mountain peaks of truth ; and no other part of the Bible more fully and clearly relates all these things to the life of the nation, and even to the things of the material world, even to the inanimate world.

In approaching this Epistle the writer always seems to hear a voice saying " Put off thy shoes from off thy feet for the place whereon thou standest is holy ground."

With reverence, then, let us approach the study of this letter from " Our Father " which is " in Heaven " ; viz. : The Epistle to the Hebrews.

The Statesmanship of Jesus

A Study in the wonderful Epistle to the Hebrews
By THE REV. W. PASCOE GOARD

CHAPTER I
PERSONAL REPENTANCE.

" Therefore leaving the principles of the doctrine of Christ, let us go on unto perfection ; not laying again the foundation . . . and this will we do, if God permit " (Heb. vi, 1 and 3).

BEFORE " going on " it will be well that we should inspect the foundation " principles," and make sure that each of the six foundation courses are " well and truly laid."

The foundation is given to us as consisting of six courses of masonry. They are as follows (Heb. vi, 1-3) :

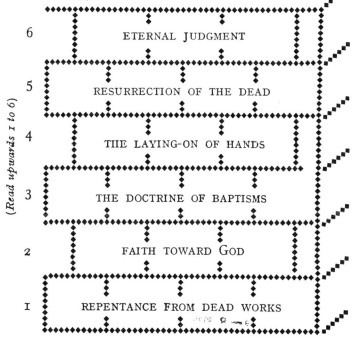

6   ETERNAL JUDGMENT

5   RESURRECTION OF THE DEAD

4   THE LAYING-ON OF HANDS

3   THE DOCTRINE OF BAPTISMS

2   FAITH TOWARD GOD

1   REPENTANCE FROM DEAD WORKS

(Read upwards 1 to 6)

The courses of masonry are massive. The outline of the building as marked out by the foundation is large and imposing. But it must be seen and remembered that the whole intention of the lines thus mentioned is to furnish *the foundation of a building to be erected* in its entirety upon it, to which we are urged to " go on."

To build without a proper foundation is to incur the strictures of Our Lord in His peroration at the close of the Sermon on the Mount : " And every one that heareth these sayings of mine, and doeth them not, shall be likened unto a foolish man, which built his house upon the sand : and the rain descended, and the floods came, and the winds blew, and beat upon that house ; and it fell : and great was the fall of it."

We shall in later chapters, under the caption of " Christian Perfection," consider the structure which the Great Architect has planned to be built upon this foundation. But lest the Lord should class us with the foolish men who build upon the sand, we will look closely at the details of the plan of the foundation as here outlined for us.

Course 1 of the foundation is :

" *Repentance from dead works.*"

We should all be glad if this task of repentance, this initial part of the task, were not laid upon us. Repentance is an unwelcome business when and wherever it is met with. But inasmuch as it is the initial step to the building of our " House not made with hands, eternal in the heavens," we will face it and make the necessary beginning.

PERSONAL REPENTANCE

" Repentance from dead works."

We shall view this from the standpoint of our individual, Church, and national relationship to God.

Personal Repentance.

First, then, as to personal repentance in our relationship to the Church. Let it be understood that when we use the word " Church " we are not referring to any man-made organisation, but to that spiritual and heavenly organisation which includes *all known to the Lord as the members of His body*.

What are to be classed as dead works?

Everything which is done for the sake and purpose of securing the salvation of our souls thereby. It is not within the reach or scope of any works of ours to secure thereby the salvation of our souls.

This is the case when we think of *actions done in the community*, such as alms-giving, and works of social uplift for the people. Nothing that we have done, nothing that we can do, can even contribute to the salvation of our souls. " By grace ye are saved through faith, and that not of yourselves ; it is the gift of God."

Anything that we do *in the way of worship with the object and for the purpose of securing the salvation of our souls* by such acts of worship, can be nothing other than " dead works." Ages of sacrifice ; oceans of the blood of slain beasts ; lifetimes of prayers and forms of worship ; all these and every other act, depended upon for the salvation of our souls, is nothing short of dead works ; there can be no ultimate salvation in them. And because there can be no salvation in them, they are declared obnoxious to God when so offered instead of the One Great Sacrifice.

Our Lord by Himself, and with no help from any man, purged our sins ; and it is the uttermost presumption for any man, or school of men, or church composed of men and women, to thrust themselves into this task. It is the prerogative and the glory of Our Lord alone.

Thus the Mosaic ritual is done away. " There remains no more sacrifice for sin." " Once in the end of the world Christ appeared to put away sin by the sacrifice of Himself," and the sinner cannot aid in the great task of putting sin away.

Is there, then, no work and no worship demanded of the sinner ? Yes ; and the first act of such worship is " Repentance from dead works." Work and worship are required of the Christian *who has accepted salvation as the free gift of God to the uttermost of his power, and to the last moment of his life.* " I beseech you, therefore, brethren, by the mercies of God, that ye present your bodies a living sacrifice, holy, acceptable unto God, which is your reasonable service."

The citizen cannot by his own work cause himself to be enrolled as a soldier. *That position is the gift of the King.* When by royal appointment he has become a soldier, *then his tasks begin.* He does not drill himself and equip himself to cause himself to be enrolled as a soldier. He is drilled and employed in military matters because he is a soldier. Thus it is with the sinner. He does not work and worship to save his soul thereby. But, having accepted the grace which saves as a gift from God, *from that moment he is face to face with his duties as a Christian.*

REPENTANCE FOR THE CHURCH ; ORGANIC.

John Wesley rediscovered the fact that there is a psychological and spiritual experience which enables the sinner to know *that he is justified in the presence of God,* and is saved from his sins and their consequences. That is to say, he is able to know that *he has received the free gift of God, which is salvation.* He is made aware of it by spiritual means. It is the testimony of the leaders of our nation that John Wesley's rediscovery and insistent preaching of this fact not only brought triumphant gladness to those who entered into that consciousness, but *saved the nation as a nation* from the over-flowing of the French Revolution, and by doing so saved Western civilisation from extinction. It is the testimony of present Cabinet ministers and other leaders of Britain that what the present day needs is another John Wesley.

Why should this generation need another John Wesley ? Precisely because the Church as an organisation in all its branches *has largely ceased to preach that doctrine, and has gone back to the preaching of dead works ;* namely, of works and of forms and ceremonies of worship for the purpose of securing salvation.

17

Therefore, as to individual members of the Church, and as to the Church at large, we must lay anew the foundation, " *Repentance from dead works.*"

NATIONAL REPENTANCE.

The nation as a nation, and every citizen within it, must also lay this first course of the foundation, " Repentance from dead works."

What are dead works considered nationally ?

Planning and doing things merely with the avowed and real object of securing the nation's prosperity ? Like salvation, this latter also is *the gift of God's grace.* Our national and international efforts outside of God's revealed plan always have failed in history, and always must fail.

It will, however, be the most simple method to put *the positive side*, the things which the nation should do ; then to see how far away the nation is from doing these things, and how fearfully busy she is in doing other things which can but be classed as " dead works." When we use the term " nation," we mean the Celto-Saxon peoples at large, the " nation and company of nations."

First, *God established the nation as the basis of His Kingdom*, and as His " special treasure." Let this fact sink well into our minds as the first positive thing we would say regarding the things that matter. This is the fundamental national fact. Britain, the Overseas Dominions, and the United States, will never get anywhere as to peace and tranquillity until each and all together realise that collectively the race is Divinely appointed to be *the Kingdom nation of the Lord.* We are of the impression that God looks upon all these nations as one entity. He organised the twelve tribes of Israel into one nation, which later should become a company of nations, with the declaration, " Ye shall be unto Me a Kingdom."

The next thing we must call to mind is that Jehovah the LORD has *established Himself for ever as King in Israel* ; that is to say, as to modern times, in the Celto-Saxon Kingdom.

This thought must sink down into our hearts, into our legislatures, into our national Cabinets, into the heads and staffs of our administrative departments. The LORD Jehovah is our King in very deed, and as nations we must know and do His will. No Act may be passed, nor order issued by Council or by Court, which will not honour His presence and His Kingship. *Every step in the administration of our country must be worthy of Him, inasmuch as they become His acts* ; that is to say, *the acts of His Government.*

Let this fact once get home to the minds and hearts of our people, and our national activities will take on another spirit.

Again, we must remember as a most matter-of-fact basis of national activity, that the LORD has given to us *a national Constitution*, perfect in every part. This consists of the Commandments, Statutes and Judgments of Jehovah. Of these, David, the great administrator, said, " The law of Jehovah is perfect, converting the soul." Let it be remembered that he was no nomadic tribal leader, but the King of a nation which could put a million fighting men in the field. Let us remember that, under the impulse and guidance of that Constitution, David and his son Solomon extended the bounds of his home kingdom from the Mediterranean to the Euphrates, made this nation the leading power in the earth, both militarily and culturally, and *extended colonial and commercial enterprise over the northern hemisphere,* laying foundations which have never been uprooted to this day.

Now God gave to the nation the duty and privilege of administering that Constitution, and of demonstrating its principles and power to the ends of the earth.

But the Lord Jehovah withheld the right and authority from the nation to add to, take from, or to amend that Constitution. Its sole right was to administer it. This was the nation's glory, as the Bible most clearly tells us; and this was the nation's salvation.

But God's Kingdom nation has committed and is perpetrating horrible transgressions. *The nation has ignored and forgotten the fact that Jehovah is really the King of the nation.* Perfunctorily we assure Him that such is the case in our national service. With lip service we thus draw near to Him still. But in heart and practice we have forgotten and deny the fact of His Kingship in the nation. We do not think of it in the courts.

The judge does not think of himself as the " alter ego " of the King who " sits upon the throne of Jehovah," as David did, and Solomon. The "counsel learned in the law " of the court do not as a profession realise that they are there as *ministers of Jehovah*, to see righteousness established, and to see that no wrong is done to any man, especially to the innocent man. The courts have forgotten that it is the glory of the King of Israel to " forgive iniquity, transgression, and sin." When a barrister goes into the court robed in his priestly robes, for that is really what he wears, to " secure a conviction," he fails to remember that he is the minister of Him who said, " Neither do I condemn thee," even though He, best of all men, knew the flagrancy of the transgression of the sinner brought before Him.

The nation has forgotten and ignores the fact that Jehovah is the established Head of every commercial and industrial organisation, and that all transactions come under His eye and administration. The nation forgets that the commercial magnate who wields less or more power stands in the place of the Lord among those with whom he deals.

The worker forgets that " *to the Lord* " he is rendering service from day to day ; that *to the Lord* he is ultimately responsible ; that *from the Lord* he will receive reward for his labours in field, factory or office, or that *from the Lord* he will meet condemnation or reward.

We must repent as a nation from a host of dead works herein.

The nation has put away the Commandments, Statutes and Judgments of the Lord, and has established her own laws. This has been the case from the time of Omri, King of Israel.

We are all equally guilty here ; and our own action has brought its own fearful punishment. What strivings, what tumults, what wars, have been our portion. If it had not been for the mercy and long-suffering of Our Lord and King we should long ago have perished from the face of the land. But the Lord has had long mercy, and is now *calling the nation to repentance and the restoration of His law.* He pledges His Word in the New Covenant that He will bring this about.

National repentance will bring about the restoration of the Divine law and the return of the knowledge, and the glad realisation of the facts which will follow the knowledge, that Jehovah reigneth in Israel-Britain still.

Thus individually, ecclesiastically and nationally, as to individual, Church and State, the foundation course of masonry must be " Repentance from dead works."

CHAPTER II

" Faith toward God "

This matter *would seem* to be so well understood that it is unnecessary to write regarding it, but is it indeed so? Has the present generation heard very much about the doctrine of Faith towards God? We doubt it very much.

True, there still remain circles which place faith among the doctrines essential to individual and community life. But this is usually presented as simply faith in Our Lord Jesus Christ as our personal Saviour. This teaching is true, gloriously true, *but it is not all*. The great foundation of Faith towards God has a much wider scope than this view of it would convey.

If we would take the full meaning and the full power of this foundation doctrine, we must still keep to our dual consideration of what I may call *faith national* and *faith ecclesiastical*. Not two objectives for our thoughts, but two phases of one great doctrine.

Faith towards God! Faith towards God!! Faith towards God!!! Let the words ring in our minds and hearts as we approach the matter.

That faith is essential to the Christian life we all agree. But what is that faith? In what terms is it to be expressed? In what realm or realms is it to be worked out? These are vital questions if we would understand the foundation of Christian doctrine.

" What saith the Scriptures ? ' *Abraham believed God ;* and it was counted to him for righteousness.' "

Many believe *in God*—that is to say, they believe that God is—who do not believe the Word which He has spoken. They believe *in* Him ; but they do not believe *Him.*

Many even believe *on God,* perhaps to the saving of their souls ; but they do not believe Him *in the Word which He has spoken.* There are words spoken by Him which they do believe, of course, otherwise they would not believe on Him ; but there are many things spoken of Him that they do not positively believe, even though they may not positively disbelieve.

The foundation faith of which we speak to-day *goes the whole way.* It is in the widest sense Faith towards God ; Faith in Him ; Faith on Him ; Faith in His spoken word.

By what means does God speak to us that we may believe ? He spake " at sundry times and in divers manners in time past unto the fathers by the prophets." He " hath in these last days spoken unto us by His Son."

That is to say, He has spoken unto us by the prophets of the Old Testament, and by the voice of the Lord in the New Testament. This is the Message we have from God.

What is it that God has spoken and that we must believe ?

The story is a straightforward one. It is one story, the various parts of which were spoken " at sundry times and in divers manners " over a period of more than a thousand years.

It begins with the story of the Creation. It proceeds to the story of the beginning of Adamic life on earth. It follows the redemption line down through Seth and Shem to Abraham, Isaac and Jacob.

It presents the Covenants made with these in their fullness.

It tells of the family of Israel going down into Egypt. It tells of their emergence from Egypt. It tells of their organisation into a nation. It tells of the organisation of their worship, and of the organisation of their national life. It reveals the law of the nation. It tells of their induction into their own land. It tells of the establishment of the Lord therein as King, and tells how He administered the law of the nation through the Judges. It tells of the establishment of the Kingdom of David. It follows the history of the people.

It records *the covenants, the promises,* and proceeds to the prophecies.

It reveals God's plan for the salvation of the souls of men, and for the establishment of righteousness in the earth by means of national organisation and administration. It tells of the lands Israel should possess, and of the fact that for ages she should forfeit some of these lands. It tells of the division of the nation into two, and

what tribes made up each. It tells of the captivities
and of their duration—that of Judah seventy
years ; that of Israel two thousand five hundred
and twenty years. It tells of Israel divorced from
God, and sent out into captivity, there to wander
for ages through the wilderness. It tells in the
meantime of a daughter state called " Israel in the
Isles." It tells of the fact that the throne of David
should be established there. It tells of the rise of
the continental nations, and of the succession and
duration of them. It tells of their overthrow, and
of Israel's restoration in the latter days. It tells
of Israel's colonial enterprise and of her colonising
the ends of the earth. It tells of her freeing the
slave, and gathering the heathen under her flag.
It tells of the coming of the Messiah as *the
Saviour of the world,* and as *the Redeemer of Israel.*
It tells of His ministry, of His betrayal, and of His
death. It tells how much he should be sold for,
and what should eventually be done with the
money for which He was sold. It tells of the
soldiers playing a game of hazard at the foot of
His Cross, and that they would cast lots for His
garment. It tells of His death, burial, resurrection
and ascension. All these things were told pro-
phetically ages before He was born. *The history*
of His birth, and of all that pertained to His life,
we have in the Gospels. The meaning of it all
we have in the Epistles. And finally we have the
pre-written history in the Book of Revelation, of
His activities during the Christian dispensation
from the national standpoint, and the culmina-

tion of the teaching that He should in due time come again and take the throne of His father David in Israel.

It tells of the great wars of the nations, who should struggle against the rule of the world going into the hands of His Kingdom-nation Israel, and finally against its going into His own hands.

It tells of the final triumph of the nation Israel, and through Israel, in which the rule of Jehovah is still going on, the restoration of all things.

Such in part is the outline of the great story.

In later days we have dissevered the story of the atoning work of the Lord from the story of the Kingdom message, and have presented it alone as the object and ground of our faith.

This must now be reversed, and our faith must reach out to the full doctrine of the Lord. Faith towards God must include the great doctrines which form the " plan of salvation," and they must also include the great doctrines which form the basis of the Divine administration of the affairs of the nation.

For any man or any school to deny that Jehovah, our Omniscient King, has left Himself without a plan to work to in either of these great departments of His administration, or that He has failed to make it known to those of whom He has declared, " Now ye are labourers together with God," is to show a very low estimate of Divine wisdom, and a very poor grasp of the great facts which underlie all individual and national experience in Israel. Let us set forth the outline of faith as to the plan of salvation.

First, the diagnosis of the health of the person to be saved, furnished by the Lord, must be accepted. Our own knowledge of all the symptoms will aid us in accepting the Divine conclusion.

" The whole head is sick, and the whole heart faint. From the sole of the foot even unto the head there is no soundness in it ; but wounds, and bruises, and putrefying sores : they have not been closed, neither bound up, neither mollified with ointment " (Isa. i, 5, 6).

" There is none that doeth good ; no, not one."

With many variations the same great truth is sent home to the minds of those who will read and understand. The patient is sick and dying. It is but a question of a short time until the life will expire, unless there be Divine remedies provided; for helpless is the aid of man.

Thus we get the great doctrine of sin permeating the human family so that none may escape. When we have mastered the secrets of biology, of physiology, and of pathology, we shall understand how terribly true this is. Leading physicians and men of physiological and biological science know that the race is corrupt in body and in the conscious and subconscious mind.

We must now accept the remedy provided. It is, the application by faith of the precious BLOOD OF CHRIST, " the Lamb of God which taketh away the sin of the world."

There must be faith in the vivifying power of the blood of Christ. *Thus far in the realm of biology.*

In the realm of jurisprudence we must accept *the legal justification* before the bar of eternal justice, which is brought about by the fact of the substitutionary sufferings of Our Lord. " All we like sheep have gone astray ; we have turned every one to his own way ; *and the Lord hath laid on Him the iniquity of us all."*

Those who put away the great doctrine of the Atonement remove the faith course from the foundation, and thus endanger the whole edifice.

UPLIFT IN THE SCALE OF BEING.

He must believe in *the regeneration of the life of man ;* i.e., the re-birth into a higher order. There is not the slightest evidence that one species ever evolved into another species of a higher order. But there is abundant evidence that God gives to the sons of Adam, who are " of the earth earthy," the power to become the Sons of God. This is not by process of evolution, but by an act of Divine inbreathing of life. " To as many as received Him, to them gave He power to become the Sons of God ; which were born . . . of God "—the new birth by the Holy Spirit.

This is the triumph of human life. It is missed entirely and for ever by the practical evolutionist, who dreams away life's great opportunity in the fond but fatal hope that the inherent powers of life will do for him what nothing but the personally-applied creative, regenerative power of God can do ; and which God accomplishes by the agency of faith.

Thus he must review the great principles of the Christian faith as set forth in the Bible, and make them the road by which he shall ascend to God.

But what of the faith of the nation?

The very first matter of faith for the nation is the racial Covenant granted by El Shaddai (God Almighty) to Abraham, Isaac, and Jacob ; and the next matter of faith is the NATIONAL COVENANT granted by the Lord Jehovah to the nation Israel.

The person or school who looks at generalities for this will inevitably go far astray. The covenants which lie at the base of the nation's life are granted to Israel, and to Israel alone.

There are other branches of the human family to whom other covenants have been from time to time granted. These they have possessed and expended, as their history shows. With such covenants *we as a race and nation* have nothing to do. They were not granted to us, nor to our nation. We never were and never shall be parties to them. For instance, the covenant granted to Ishmael : and the covenant granted to the continental Empires, as set forth in the second and other chapters of Daniel.

What is material to us is *the specific covenants granted to Israel of the twelve tribes ; to Israel of the ten tribes ; and to the House of David in conjunction with Israel.*

The racial Covenant made with the Fathers we have inherited. (Gen. xvi.)

The first covenant granted to the nation at Sinai we received as a race, abused and lost. That covenant was broken by us and disregarded by God. This fact is set forth in the thirty-first chapter of Jeremiah and in the eighth chapter of Hebrews, and elsewhere.

The New Covenant made with ten-tribed Israel is ours to-day. Nothing can remove it. It does not depend upon our action towards it. It is based firmly upon the " I will " and " They shall " of God. This is a better covenant, founded upon better promises, and it is ours to-day—thank God! (See Jer. xxxi).

The *covenant renewed with the House of David* at the very time that the House of David seemed to be in the act of disappearing from history, as recorded in the thirty-third chapter of Jeremiah, is ours, for it is made with the House of David in conjunction with the House of Israel. (See Jer. xxxiii).

These covenants convey to us the assurance of *the restoration of the law of God in the minds and hearts of the nation, the perpetuation of the nation to the end of time,* and *the restoration of Jerusalem the late and the coming capital of the nation. The renewed covenant with the House of David provides for the permanence of the Davidic reign in Israel for ever.*

These and similar things are granted in covenants and confirmed by the oath of God, that by " two immutable things, in which it was impossible for God to lie, we might have a strong consolation."

These are matters of " Faith towards God," which form in part the foundation of Christian faith ; and it is for us to see whether we have been exercising that faith or not.

The *national promises* and the *national prophecies* are just as clearly set forth as the ground of our faith, and the challenge to our faith. But we cannot pursue that matter further. Their united fulfilment demonstrates the validity of covenants, promises, prophecies, and of the Scriptures generally.

The next great field of Faith towards God is *the* REDEMPTION *of the nation Israel.* Mark, while there is an individual element in the Redemption, *chiefly it is a national matter.* Do not confuse the Redemption with the Atonement. The Atonement is for the sin of the individual, and of the people as a whole. The Redemption is from the divorced condition into which Israel fell, and is for the citizenship of the nation ; it is also and primarily for the nation as an organised whole. Read Isaiah xlix-liv with the thought of the nation in mind. Especially read chapter liv for *the result of the Redemption,* and see that it is a national result.

Why is this ? *Because the nation is the basis of God's Kingdom, and of God's administration among the nations, and He requires the service of the nation in that field of Divine activity.* Therefore, the nation must not be allowed to perish for its sins. Christ redeemed the nation on Calvary ; *therefore* it stands for ever. Thank God for such a RE-

DEMPTION, which we are all assured the nation in no sense deserved.

The Redemption is offered as a ground and challenge of Faith towards God.

Again, and this is the last we have time to mention : *The Second Coming of Our Lord, to reign in and over His Kingdom nation, is offered unmistakably as a ground and challenge to our faith.*

From the ecclesiastical standpoint there seems to be no good reason for the return of the Lord. We are not at all surprised that many of those who deal exclusively with the doctrines of salvation should not accept the teaching regarding the Second Coming of Our Lord. Let such ask themselves the question : " Is not my faith halting here because I am not at all informed, or only partly informed, as to the national Kingly work undertaken, and to be completed, by Our Lord ? " *His priestly work of sacrifice is finished.* In this we glory. *His Kingly work on earth is not yet begun.* The Kingdom must yet receive the incarnate King. The King must return to finish His Kingly work. Once these kindred facts are seen, doubt as to the Second Coming of Our Lord must for ever pass from the mind.

The " Faith towards God," as we have seen, embraces the acceptance of the Covenants, Promises, Prophecies, Atoning work, and Redemptive sacrifice. It is a glorious field which challenges our faith, and furnishes a course of foundation masonry worthy of the great Master Builder " Who is the author and the finisher of our faith."

CHAPTER III

THE DOCTRINE OF BAPTISMS

IN the last two chapters we have been following the epitome of the foundation of Christian doctrines as they are presented in the Epistle to the Hebrews, chapter vi, 1-3.

In the first we presented a figure illustrating the presentation of the foundation, showing six courses of masonry, and thereafter considered the first course of masonry in the foundation, namely, " Repentance from dead works."

In the second chapter we considered briefly the second course of masonry in the foundation, namely, " Faith towards God."

We shall now glance at the third course of masonry in the foundation, namely, " The Doctrine of Baptisms."

Let us note that the term is in the plural. It is not the question of baptism, but of baptisms, washings.

Let us call to mind the question of the Catechism : " What is baptism ? " and then let us remember the answer : " Baptism is an outward and visible sign of an inward and spiritual grace."

This seems to be a very good definition of the first baptism—that of water.

Then comes the question : " Who are the proper subjects of baptism ? " The answer to this must not be drawn from the Catechism, but from the statements of the Word of God.

Taking them in the order they seem to occur in the Scriptures, we make answer :

1. The Nation.
2. The Church.
3. The Individual.

Perhaps we shall all agree in the matter thus far presented ; and we desire to avoid that field of study in regard to the matter which is a subject of controversy. Only the plain facts regarding the matter of baptism will be here touched upon.

What is the element of baptism ?

1. Water.
2. Holy Spirit.
3. Fire.

These are the elements of baptism.

Let us now consider the facts of baptism as we read them in the Scriptures.

THE INDIVIDUAL.

John the Baptist taught baptism in relation to the ministry of Our Lord. John's baptism was of water. His call was to repentance.

The baptism of John was that of the forerunner. His " Baptisma " was introductory to that of Christian baptism as taught by the Apostle Paul, which is set forth in the statement which follows in connection with the baptism with the Holy Ghost. See Acts xix, 1-7.

The implication of baptism, the point it symbolises, at which the candidate becomes " united with Him " (marginal reading) is set forth in the sixth chapter of Romans, from which we quote the following :

Rom. vi, 1-11 :

What shall we say then ? Shall we continue in sin, that grace may abound ?

God forbid. How shall we, that are dead to sin, live any longer therein ?

Know ye not, that so many of us as were baptized into Jesus Christ were baptized into his death ?

Therefore we are buried with him by baptism into death : that like as Christ was raised up from the dead by the glory of the Father, even so we also should walk in newness of life.

For if we have been planted together in the likeness of his death, we shall be also *in the likeness* of *his* resurrection :

Knowing this, that our old man is crucified with *him,* that the body of sin might be destroyed, that henceforth we should not serve sin.

For he that is dead is freed from sin.

Now if we be dead with Christ, we believe that we shall also live with him :

Knowing that Christ being raised from the dead dieth no more ; death hath no more dominion over him.

For in that he died, he died unto sin once : but in that he liveth, he liveth unto God.

Likewise reckon ye also yourselves to be dead indeed unto sin, but alive unto God through Jesus Christ our Lord.

The signification of the rite of baptism was the washing away of sin, and symbolises union and identification with our Lord.

One might well ask the question : Why should there be the outward ceremonial ministration of water, when it is certain that *the ministration of water cannot wash away sin* ? In replying to this question we must take cognisance of the process by which the communicant or candidate for baptism is lifted, by regenerating grace, aside from the rite of baptism, from that limited state which the Apostle Paul in the second chapter of the first Epistle to the Corinthians calls " the natural man," which *cannot perceive the things of the spirit*, to that higher state called in the same chapter " he which is spiritual." In the stage of a person's experience which Paul terms the " natural man " it is useless to call upon him for the exercise of that vision which sees the spiritual. "He cannot see the Kingdom of God." At that stage of his experience, and up to the moment of regeneration, *spiritual vision is non-existent in his experience. He can neither see, nor enter into the things of the spirit.* But *he can reason regarding them.* He can read the promises in the written Word. He can in a measure understand the doctrines therein which present spiritual things. He can even *believe in them* for himself. But he cannot see, and he cannot experience them. The inner and spiritual grace which regenerates and cleanses from sin he may accept as a doctrine. He may even believe it as an act of faith. But he cannot see the process, nor know it as a matter of personal experience at this stage. Therefore he must show his faith by symbol. The symbol prepared to meet his material vision at this point is that of the ministration of water. He believes the promises as written, as a *mental process*. He applies for baptism as *an act of faith*.

He knows that he is baptized with the symbolic element, and *he believes* that the inward and spiritual grace is applied to him, even though he *cannot know* it as an experience at the time. Thus having *believed*, and having acted, he awaits the assurance of Divine Grace.

The waters of baptism are ministered to him at the very threshold of the spiritual life he is being called upon to enter, and symbolises but does not constitute the essential requisite, as he is about by regeneration to enter into the Body of Our Lord. It is a symbol only, outward and physical, of an inward and spiritual grace experienced or desired.

Thus the element is ministered, and this is the thing signified thereby.

Still following the thought of the individual, we come to the second essential of baptism, namely, the baptism with the Holy Spirit. Perhaps the best illustration of this is contained in the narrative of the experience of the Apostle Paul at Ephesus (Acts xix, 1-7) :

And it came to pass, that, while Apollos was at Corinth, Paul having passed through the upper. coasts came to Ephesus : and finding certain disciples,

He said unto them, Have ye received the Holy Ghost since ye believed ? And they said unto him, We have not so much as heard whether there be any Holy Ghost.

And he said unto them, Unto what then were ye baptized ? And they said, Unto John's baptism.

Then said Paul, John verily baptized with the baptism of repentance, saying unto the people, that they should believe on him which should come after him, that is, on Christ Jesus.

When they heard this, they were baptized in the *name of the Lord Jesus.*

And when Paul had laid his hands upon them, the Holy Ghost came on them ; and they spake with tongues, and prophesied.

And all the men were about twelve.

We have not space at this point to discuss at length the baptism of the Holy Ghost. We see that it is a fact in the experience of Christians ; and that it should be a fact in the experience of all. This seems to be the expectation of the Apostle Paul, and the specific teaching is that " the manifestation of the Spirit is given to every man to profit withal."

We also see that this is not a symbolic rite, but a veritable experience. There is no outward and visible sign of this inward and spiritual grace, but there is the matter-of-fact reception of the enduement of the Holy Ghost.

Still pursuing the individual experience, we come to *the baptism with power,* or with fire : " Ye shall receive power after that the Holy Ghost has come upon you . . ." We shall not labour this point. We simply point it out as an accepted fact of the foundation doctrines of baptisms.

Let us now look at the matter of *baptism for the Church at large.* This is best illustrated by the Pentecost narrative in the second chapter of the Acts of the Apostles. Speaking of the infant Church of Christ we read (Acts ii, 1-4) : " And when the day of Pentecost was fully come, they were all with one accord in one place. And suddenly there came a sound from heaven as of a rushing mighty wind, and it *filled all the house* where they were sitting. And there appeared unto them cloven tongues like as of fire, and it sat upon each of them. And they *were all filled* with the Holy Ghost, and began to speak with other tongues, as the Spirit gave them utterance."

Acts xi, 13-18 :

And he shewed us how he had seen an angel in his house, which stood and said to him, Send men to Joppa, and call for Simon, whose surname is Peter ;

Who shall tell thee words, whereby thou and all thy house shall be saved.

And as I began to speak, the Holy Ghost fell on them, as on us at the beginning.

Then remembered I the word of the Lord, how that he said, John indeed baptized with water ; but ye shall be baptized with the Holy Ghost.

Forasmuch then as God gave them the like gift as he did unto us, who believed on the Lord Jesus Christ ; what was I, that I could withstand God ?

When they heard these things, they held their peace, and glorified God, saying, Then hath God also to the Gentiles granted repentance unto life.

Thus we see that there is a baptism for the Church as a whole, who are assembled together in long-continued worship.

One must bear in mind the Holy Ghost the third Person of the Holy Trinity, and the Holy Spirit proceeding from the Trinity with which God's people are baptized.

BAPTISM OF THE NATION.

Now for the moment let us look at a comparatively forgotten phase of baptism, namely, *the baptism of the nation*, the Kingdom-nation Israel. Note that this latter is not a general doctrine for all nations. The facts we have looked upon as to the individual are for all the sons of Adam who accept Christ. The facts of which we have spoken concerning the Church are for the Church of Christ wherever it is found, in Israel or out among " the kingdoms of this world." But the fact of national baptism seems to be guaranteed to Israel alone. There is always a good and sufficient reason for this national limitation. The reason being that God said to Israel alone as a nation : " Ye shall be unto me a kingdom of Priests."

The illustrations of this great phase of this doctrine of baptisms we have selected are, first, in I Cor. x. "Our fathers...... were all *baptized unto Moses* in the cloud and in the sea." Thus Israel was delivered from the power of Egypt, and brought into national fellowship with God at Sinai. The second is an experience yet future for the nation as set forth in the thirty-sixth chapter of Ezekiel. This speaks of *the nation* in the latter days, under the New Covenant, in active preparation for the coming of the King (Ezekiel xxxvi, 16-38) :

Moreover the word of the Lord came unto me, saying,

Son of man, when the house of Israel dwelt in their own land, they defiled it by their own way and by their doings : their way was before me as the uncleanness of a removed woman.

Wherefore I poured my fury upon them for the blood that they had shed upon the land, and for their idols wherewith they had polluted it :

And I scattered them among the heathen, and they were dispersed through the countries : according to their way and according to their doings I judged them.

And when they entered unto the heathen, whither they went, they profaned my holy name, when they said to them, These are the people of the Lord, and are gone forth out of his land.

But I had pity for mine holy name, which the house of Israel had profaned among the heathen, whither they went.

Therefore say unto the house of Israel, Thus saith the Lord God ; I do not this for your sakes, O house of Israel, but for mine holy name's sake, which ye have profaned among the heathen, whither ye went.

And I will sanctify my great name, which was profaned among the heathen, which ye have profaned in the midst of them ; and the heathen shall know that I am the Lord, saith the Lord God, when I shall be sanctified in you before their eyes.

For I will take you from among the heathen, and gather you out of all countries, and will bring you into your own land.

Then will I sprinkle clean water upon you, and ye shall be clean : from all your filthiness, and from all your idols, will I cleanse you.

A new heart also will I give you, and a new spirit will I put within you : and I will take away the stony heart out of your flesh, and I will give you an heart of flesh.

And I will put my spirit within you, and cause you to walk in my statutes, and ye shall keep my judgments, and do them.

And ye shall dwell in the land that I gave to your fathers ; and ye shall be my people, and I will be your God.

I will also save you from all your uncleannesses : and I will call for the corn, and will increase it, and lay no famine upon you.

And I will multiply the fruit of the tree, and the increase of the field, that ye shall receive no more reproach of famine among the heathen.

Then shall ye remember your own evil ways, and your doings that were not good, and shall lothe yourselves in your own sight for your iniquities and for your abominations.

Not for your sakes do I this, saith the Lord God, be it known unto you : be ashamed and confounded for your own ways, O house of Israel.

Thus saith the Lord God ; In the day that I shall have cleansed you from all your iniquities I will also cause you to dwell in the cities, and the wastes shall be builded.

And the desolate land shall be tilled, whereas it lay desolate in the sight of all that passed by.

And they shall say, This land that was desolate is become like the garden of Eden ; and the waste and desolate and ruined cities are become fenced, and are inhabited.

Then the heathen that are left round about you shall know that I the Lord build the ruined places, and plant that that was desolate : I the Lord have spoken it, and I will do it.

Thus saith the Lord God : I will yet for this be enquired of by the house of Israel, to do it for them ; I will increase them with men like a flock.

As the holy flock, as the flock of Jerusalem in her solemn feasts ; so shall the waste cities be filled with flocks of men ; and they shall know that I am the Lord.

The nation thus cleansed shall be made ready for the coming of the King, and the closer administration of His will. Hitherto Israel has been carrying on in semi-blindness. Unconsciously and blindly she has been constrained to carry out the higher purposes of Jehovah, the God and King of Israel. This has been manifested at home in the great reforms and in the great defence waged again and again of the fundamental laws of the State as in Magna Charta, and so on. Always Britain and her daughter nations will arise when the great principles of the Divine constitution are really endangered, and will fight anew one way or another the battle of freedom.

Again it is seen in the great principles which dominate the foreign policy of Britain. How little statesmanship and politics have had to do with the forward march of Britain's foreign policy. Against the will and interest of Parties she has carried forward an unswerving policy of principle, and has forced results little expected by the statesmen which brought the matter about. The underlying trend of foreign policy throughout British history illustrates what is meant.

Again, *it is manifested in the treatment secured and granted to the subject races.* How has Britain spent life, blood and treasure for the uplift and liberation of the down-trodden! The politicians have shouted and screamed against these things generation after generation. But still they have been carried on. Parties have gone to the country and have won elections on the strength of promises to sever Britain from the task and the expense. But even Parties so elected have found themselves obliged to carry on often deeper than ever by a Power they could not control.

But the time is coming when she shall be baptized with Spirit power as Israel was under Moses, and shall be fitted for the task which shall be her choice with open vision.

Having been thus sanctified, there comes to the nation the renewed investiture with the Jehovah Name and power as we have spoken at length under the caption " The Sealing of Israel " in *The National Message and Banner,* dated Sept. 18th, 1926.*

For the individual and for the nation baptism has each a place and purpose.

Baptism with water is for the washing away of sin, profession of conviction, and faith and for the entering upon the life ministry.

Baptism with the Holy Ghost is for the enrichment of the experience and for equipment for service.

The baptism of the nation is for identification, consecration and for service, to be perfected by endowment with the Jehovah Name.

What a wonderfully rich field is the study of " Baptism," and how well it will repay the earnest Christian for the time and effort spent in the study thereof.

* COVENANT PUBLISHING Co., 6, Buckingham Gate, London, S.W.1.

CHAPTER IV

The Laying-on of Hands

WE now proceed to examine briefly the fourth course of the foundation, namely, the doctrine of " *the laying-on of hands.*"

It will come as somewhat of a surprise to some that the doctrine of " *the laying-on of hands* " is a foundation doctrine of the Christian faith. Yet such is the case, as we see in the text before us. The results which follow the laying-on of hands are made clear in the record of the Christian ministry as set forth in the New Testament.

There are specific reasons for the laying-on of hands.

(1) *For the reception of the Holy Ghost* ; (2) *for ordination to the Christian ministry of the Word* ; and (3) *for healing of the sick.* These things we shall see clearly set forth as we proceed.

Who are those who should lay hands upon the candidate ?

For the baptism with the Holy Ghost it is manifest that those who should lay on hands for this particular ministry *must be persons who have received the baptism of the Holy Ghost,* and therefore are in a position to minister the same.

For ordination to the Christian ministry, those who hold authority in the organisation of the Christian

47

Church, and have at the same time received the baptism of the Holy Ghost.

For the ministry of healing, those who have been called of God to carry forward the Christian ministry as ordained ministers, or as " elders of the Church," and those who have the especial gift of the Holy Spirit which endows with power for such a ministry of healing.

These things seem to be manifest and obvious. There are many other things to be said in this connection which would be outside the scope of this brief chapter.

The underlying qualification for the laying-on of hands in each connection is that the ministrant shall have himself received the gift of the Holy Ghost.

What is there at the basis of this ministry ?

This question we might answer by a simple examination of the texts of Scripture which deal with the same. But perhaps we may not be losing time or effort if we go a little farther afield with our enquiry, yet remaining within the general scope of the teaching of the written Word.

The human personality is manifold. " Body and soul and spirit " are clearly marked departments of the complex life of man.

There is in the texture of the person *the atom,* which being of the dust of the earth is formed into the body of the man. " God formed man of the dust of the earth." It is interesting and important to note that this substratum of the living man is wholly composed of the homely materials of earth,

THE LAYING-ON OF HANDS

and water, and air. There is not a foreign particle to be found in it, as the analytical chemist will assure us.

The *material part*, the hand that is to be laid upon the head of the candidate, is of this homely material, " the dust of the earth," and in it there is nothing outside of the chemistry of the earth.

Now there is in the atom a force which seems not to be material. The chemist well knows that it is there and that the atom is instinct with its potentialities. He can neither separate the force from the atom nor the atom from the force.

The chemist knows that such force will attract atom to atom and so form a molecule. He knows that in the molecule so formed there is a community force not to be found in the atom alone, and that such force holds the molecule together.

He knows that the molecule attracts other molecules, arranges them into certain forms and so builds up substances, which have more or less of tensile strength and of clearly ascertained breaking strain.

The chemist knows that other elements may be introduced which will release the molecules from each other, thus destroying the fabric, and the atoms from each other, thus bringing about a new form of molecule and a new substance.

But all the foregoing, and much more, *are activities in the realm of inorganic substances.* There is in all this neither consciousness, emotion nor will.

Therefore the laying upon the head of the candidate hands which are purely material might have some little magnetic influence, but as far as the question we are studying is concerned such laying-on of hands would be without effect.

We come now to the second clause of the great passage we quoted above. The second clause reads, " and breathed into his nostrils the breath of life, and man became a living soul."

Something like this " laying-on of hands " exists in the case of the lower orders of life. The spirit and the will of the lower animals have a power of their own expressed in physical contact as is seen by the influence of one animal upon another, and by their influence upon ourselves. Thus the sympathetic touches of a faithful dog have brought comfort to many a man and boy, to many a woman and child in distress. How much more is this the case in the life of that man of whom it was so written, " God breathed into his nostrils the breath of life, and man became a living soul " ?

Note that such inbreathing *affects every atom, every molecule, every cell of his whole being,* and is the living indwelling ego inhabiting the material atoms of the body. How this spirit manifests itself in the life of man is a matter of constant and increasing interest to the biologist, to whose mind the wonders of living tissues and living persons open up their secrets. Such a *fund and such a force of psychical life indwells every person.*

This inbreathed life produces and co-ordinates the cells of the body, and keeps or attempts to keep them in harmonious working and relationship. When that end is reached there is abounding health for the person. When the inbreathed life fails of perfect success then there is illness and disease.

The overflowing life of the individual goes out to make contribution to *a general community reservoir of psychical power*. Where this is generally so there is much conscious activity in the community life of those who share in such a general stock of contributed life. Therefore, persons in greater or less numbers are to be found seeking each other's company and enjoying community life together. Thus it is in the home, the family circle which embraces many homes, the community of friendships, the Church, and the State.

The great exhibition of this community life is in the nation, which stands firmly in the strength of the psychical life of the people. The benevolent results are shown in many directions as the community acts and sends forth influences for good to men, to communities, and to nations.

In connection with this there is a laying-on of hands. What is more comforting than the touch of the mother's hand to the distressed or suffering child. What is more heartening and encouraging than the hearty grasp of the hand of a friend to a man overburdened and distressed ?

There are communities which have been brought together to use these very forces in the battle with disease and distress, and for the uplift of the individual by the combined life power of the community to which such person belongs. It is an important matter to which we do well to pay attention.

But this does not as yet touch the matter of which we are reading, namely, the laying-on of hands in connection with the Christian ministry.

The hand so laid must be more than atomic ; it must be more than psychic ; *it must be, in the very highest sense of the term, Spiritual.*

As the life which God breathed into the nostrils of man gave to him the standing of a living soul, which exceeds the inherent force of the atom, and which force energises every atom of his nature, *so by the gift of the Holy Ghost God has given to man the infusion of a life and power which is super-psychical, superhuman, which is spiritual and of the Divine.*

This is the point we must reach if, from the standpoint of the scientific observer, we would understand that of which we are reading in the passage before us, namely, the doctrine of " the laying-on of hands."

Evolution of the atomic life can never attain this essential life and power.

Evolution of the psychical can never attain this essential life and power.

As we see it so clearly and repeatedly set forth in the statements of the Scriptures before us, *this is an external life or person " received " from without, received from above, received as the gift of God.*

Thus the Apostle Paul enquires at Ephesus,

" Have ye received the Holy Ghost since ye believed ? "

The indwelling Spirit of God energises the individual to whom He is given.

The gathering together of a group of such individuals brings about an atmosphere wherein the Presence of the Holy Spirit is felt and recognised even by those who have not received that great gift of God. The possibilities for good in such a gathering are manifest to all in whatever direction such forces may be turned ; to physical healing, for instance ; to mental quickening and instruction ; or to the conveyance of the gift of the Holy Ghost. Doubtless there are many who press this matter to extremes, but we must not, because of that fact, turn away from the great truth we are now considering.

In connection with the laying-on of hands, we are now ready to apply these thoughts.

The laying-on of physical hands can profit but little. They are made up of lime, and iron, and phosphorus, and such homely chemicals. There would be a slight chemical attraction or repulsion, a slight magnetic influence, but little more.

The laying-on of the psychical hands which infuse the atomic form can and does convey the influence of the psychical life. There is a considerable exchange of influence here, as we have said, and good or ill may be the result. But from the standpoint of the laying-on of hands this will have small result, and is not the intended meaning in the facts we are considering.

The laying-on of the hands of the Spirit life, which should be instinct in the life of the person to whom has been given the Holy Ghost ; this is the thought and purpose of the study before us, and of the passages in Holy Writ which are under consideration.

It will be clear from the foregoing that the person who imposes hands must have received the Holy Ghost if he is to be the instrument through whom others shall receive that gift of God.

It will be manifest that formal functions alone cannot here meet the requirements of the case, for here we are brought into actual contact with the Infinite, the veritable Personality of the living God.

Not every officer of the Church has received the gift of the Holy Ghost. In such case it would obviously be of little import that in his office he is in direct line from those whose hands were in their day so instinct with the life of God that those upon whose heads their hands were laid received the gift of the Holy Ghost. There may be a very precious historical line established here, and as an historical thing it would be of great interest. But if in the line of descent there was one who had not received the Holy Ghost, and who laid hands on the succeeding candidates, the spiritual chain would be broken. No, *the Holy Ghost is not received through such a lengthened chain.* The hands imposed *must be directly in touch with the living spirit of God.*

The man who has been called of God to the office of the Christian ministry, who has also been advanced to high office in the Church by the confidence and veneration of his superiors and of his brethren ; who is the choice of the membership of the Church he serves ; and who has perhaps in addition been appointed by his King ; this man, *filled with the Holy Ghost,* would be the man of all men to impose hands on the candidates. But wanting all these, the simple fishermen and the simple tent-maker upon whom the Holy Ghost fell, who took the place of the High Priest and priest, were in their day, and their like are to-day, men through whom God bestowed, and will still bestow, the gift of the Holy Ghost.

Hands are thus to be laid upon the candidate *that he may receive the gift of the Holy Ghost.* This is illustrated sufficiently in the nineteenth chapter of the Acts, verses 2 and 6 : " He said unto them, Have ye received the Holy Ghost since ye believed ? . . ."

" And when Paul had laid his hands upon them, the Holy Ghost came on them ; and they spake with tongues, and prophesied."

This gift of the Holy Ghost at once fitted them for the work of preaching the Gospel. There are many gifts of the Spirit, and many manifestations of the Spirit ; but the gift of the power to preach the unsearchable riches of Christ, in the Gospel of the Kingdom and the Gospel of Salvation, outweighs them all. It is not so much the gift of the ability to speak in unknown or foreign languages, as the gift of speech which proclaims the glorious Gospel of Our Lord.

We turn now to *the laying-on of hands in ordina-*

tion to service. Of this we shall take the illustration of the ordination of deacons to the lowly task to which they were appointed, knowing that such illustration will also cover the highest forms of ordination (Acts vi, 1-7) :

And in those days, when the number of the disciples was multiplied, there arose a murmuring of the Grecians against the Hebrews, because their widows were neglected in the daily ministration.

Then the twelve called the multitude of the disciples unto them, and said, It is not reason that we should leave the word of God, and serve tables.

Wherefore, brethren, look ye out among you seven men of honest report, full of the Holy Ghost and wisdom, whom we may appoint over this business.

But we will give ourselves continually to prayer, and to the ministry of the word.

And the saying pleased the whole multitude : and they chose Stephen, a man full of faith and of the Holy Ghost, and Philip, and Prochorus, and Nicanor, and Timon, and Parmenas, and Nicolas a proselyte of Antioch :

Whom they set before the apostles : and when they had prayed, they laid their hands on them.

And the word of God increased ; and the number of the disciples multiplied in Jerusalem greatly ; and a great company of the priests were obedient to the faith.

THE LAYING-ON OF HANDS

Thus were these good men and true set apart by the "laying-on of hands" to the work of the "ministry of tables" in the Church of Christ, from which service some of them soon graduated. Especially was this the case with Stephen, the proto-martyr of glorious memory.

Let those who have been ordained to the work of the Christian ministry see to it that they are possessed with the gift of the Holy Ghost, without which their ministry will not be attended with much success. Remembering at all times that the Holy Ghost has been often given and will again be given without the imposition of human hands.

The Laying-on of Hands for the Purposes of Physical Healing.

This great matter is set forth briefly and clearly in the condensed words of Our Lord as recorded by the Evangelist St. Mark. (St. Mark xvi, 14-20.)

Afterward He appeared unto the eleven as they sat at meat, and upbraided them with their unbelief and hardness of heart, because they believed not them which had seen him after he was risen.

And he said unto them, Go ye into all the world, and preach the gospel to every creature.

He that believeth and is baptized shall be saved ; but he that believeth not shall be damned.

And these signs shall follow them that believe : In my name shall they cast out devils ; they shall speak with new tongues ;

They shall take up serpents ; and if they drink any deadly thing, it shall not hurt them ; they shall lay hands on the sick, and they shall recover.

So then after the Lord had spoken unto them, he was received up into heaven, and sat on the right hand of God.

And they went forth, and preached everywhere, the Lord working with them, and confirming the word with signs following. Amen.

The reader will turn to many other passages which set forth this phase of truth.

CHAPTER V

THE RESURRECTION OF THE DEAD

THE former studies took in the doctrines of Repentance from dead works ; Faith toward God ; the doctrine of Baptisms ; the doctrine of the laying-on of hands. To-day we are to approach the great doctrine of the *resurrection of the dead.*

Glance at the four foundation doctrines we have thus far dealt with and see that *they are in the realm of faith and practice.* Repentance, Faith, Baptism, the Laying-on of hands ; these are all attitudes of mind and heart, and actions of the candidate. Now we are called to step out into another sphere. *The resurrection is not an attitude of mind and heart ; it is not an action directed by human volition ; it steps right out into the realm of natural phenomena.*

The resurrection of the dead is not a part of evolving human life as we know it. There is no power known to science which can bring about the resurrection of the dead. Being a fact at all, it must be a fact of a higher order than the natural phenomena with which the scientific observer is acquainted.

We are asked *to believe the doctrine* of the resurrection of the dead.

More than that, we are asked to believe *the well-attested fact* of the resurrection from the dead. This latter stamps this as the most concrete of the great foundation doctrines, for it has been capable of a physical demonstration ; nay, it has been physically demonstrated.

We shall consider the resurrection of the dead from *the standpoint of doctrine.*

We shall consider the resurrection of the dead *as a phenomenon of nature* most carefully observed, and well attested.

We shall consider the resurrection as *a demonstration of the matter-of-factness of the Christian religion ;* a demonstration lacking in every other system of faith on earth.

We shall consider the resurrection of the dead as *the great hope* for the future.

We shall consider the resurrection of the dead as *one of a well-known series of natural phenomena,* without which the natural order would indeed be incomplete and faulty ; but which rounds off and perfects the work of the Creator and the studies of the sciences the field of which is the natural order of God's creation.

THE RESURRECTION OF THE DEAD AS A MATTER OF DOCTRINE.

The doctrine constituted a hope of the pre-Christian times. To show this we may quote one passage which will be sufficient for our purpose. We quote from that rich treasure-house, Job. Thus he speaks of the resurrection (Job xix, 23-27) :

Oh that my words were now written! oh that they were printed in a book!

That they were graven with an iron pen and lead in the rock for ever!

For I know that my redeemer liveth, and that he shall stand at the latter day upon the earth :

And though after my skin worms destroy this body, yet in my flesh shall I see God :

Whom I shall see for myself, and mine eyes shall behold, and not another ; though my reins be consumed within me.

In the Old Testament and in the pre-Christian times the doctrine of the resurrection from the dead was *purely a matter of faith*, the phenomenon predicted being utterly unknown in the B.C. ages. It was a faith held with fullest conviction ; but it was a faith which had received no demonstration in the realm of natural phenomena. This was the status of the matter before the resurrection of Our Lord.

But in the A.D. days of the New Testament *the resurrection took its place among scientific facts which have been demonstrated ; the ascertained and recorded resurrection of Our Lord furnishing the demonstration.*

The New Testament is alive with the doctrine of the resurrection of the dead, as we shall see as we go on. Now it is certain that the present Christian age *holds the fact of the coming resurrection much as the Old Testament age held it*, namely, *as an article of our faith*, constituting a vital part of our creed. It is preached and believed by the Church on this ground chiefly.

It is well that the doctrine should be so held.   It is not well that it should be held as a doctrine only.

THE RESURRECTION OF THE DEAD IS A PHENOMENON OF NATURE.

The resurrection from the dead has been *experienced by Jesus of Nazareth*. The fact was demonstrated to the eleven and to many others of His disciples, who knew their Lord too well to be under any doubt as to His actual Personality ; and whose testimony was clearly given.   It was resisted by the ecclesiastical authorities and by the State, was sifted by the schools, and was finally found to be absolutely unshakable. *Thus we have the attested fact of the resurrection of the dead recorded* in many ways ; by the Evangelists, in the Acts of the Apostles, and in the Epistles.

Thus the Apostle Paul epitomises in the first Epistle to the Corinthians, the fifteenth chapter, the evidence in his great discussion of the fact of the resurrection of the dead :

Moreover, brethren, I declare unto you the gospel which I preached unto you, which also ye have received, and wherein ye stand ;

By which also ye are saved, if ye keep in memory what I preached unto you, unless ye have believed in vain.

For I delivered unto you first of all that which I also received, how that Christ died for our sins according to the Scriptures :

And that he was buried, and that he rose again the third day according to the Scriptures :

And that he was seen of Cephas, then of the twelve :

After that, he was seen of above five hundred brethren at once ; of whom the greater part remain unto this present, but some are fallen asleep.

After that, he was seen of James ; then of all the apostles.

And last of all he was seen of me also, as of one born out of due time.

For I am the least of the apostles, that am not meet to be called an apostle, because I persecuted the church of God.

But by the grace of God I am what I am ; and his grace which was bestowed upon me was not in vain ; but I laboured more abundantly than they all ; yet not I, but the grace of God which was with me.

Therefore, whether it were I or they, so we preach, and so ye believed.

Now if Christ be preached that he rose from the dead, how say some among you that there is no resurrection of the dead ?

But if there be no resurrection of the dead, then is Christ not risen :

And if Christ be not risen, then is our preaching vain, and your faith is also vain.

Yea, and we are found false witnesses of God ; because we have testified of God that he raised up Christ ; whom he raised not up, if so be that the dead rise not.

For if the dead rise not, then is not Christ raised :

And if Christ be not raised, your faith is vain ; ye are yet in your sins.

Then they also which are fallen asleep in Christ are perished.

If in this life only we have hope in Christ, we are of all men most miserable.

But now is Christ risen from the dead, and become the firstfruits of them that slept.

For since by man came death, by man came also the resurrection of the dead.

For as in Adam all die, even so in Christ shall all be made alive.

But every man in his own order : Christ the firstfruits ; afterward they that are Christ's at his coming.

Then cometh the end, when he shall have delivered up the kingdom to God, even the Father ; when he shall have put down all rule and all authority and power.

For he must reign, till he hath put all enemies under his feet.

The last enemy that shall be destroyed is death.

For he hath put all things under his feet. But when he saith all things are put under him, it is manifest that he is excepted, which did put all things under him.

And when all things shall be subdued unto him, then shall the Son also himself be subject unto him that put all things under him, that God may be all in all.

THE RESURRECTION OF THE DEAD

How wonderfully the Apostle presents the resurrection as a fact, observed and attested. Not merely a doctrine to be accepted, an article of faith to be believed ; but *an attested fact not to be denied.* Thus we see the resurrection of the dead as a fact in process of accomplishment, which in due time must receive completion.

The order of the resurrection of the dead yet to be accomplished is still a matter of doctrine ; an article of faith to be believed. But the fact of the resurrection has gone beyond that stage.

In the fact of the resurrection of the dead we have *a demonstration of the Christian Faith.*

" For if Christ be not risen then is our preaching vain, and your faith is vain . . ."

" And if Christ be not raised, your faith is vain ; ye are yet in your sins.

" Then also they which are fallen asleep in Christ are perished.

" BUT NOW IS CHRIST RISEN FROM THE DEAD, AND BECOME THE FIRSTFRUITS OF THEM THAT SLEEP."

What a wonderful demonstration of the Christian faith is here. *Christ is shown to be the Son of God with power by the resurrection from the dead.*

The fact that He died, the sinless One for the guilty, is demonstrated. Had He died as a sinful man, death would have retained Him in the place of the dead, and there would have been neither Redemption for Israel nor Atonement for the sins of mankind. But, thank God, " Now is Christ risen from the dead," and the Redemption and

Atonement are sealed with His blood, and demonstrated by His resurrection.

The writer received a delegation on one occasion of outstanding men. They came to ask why he could not accept the teachings of a religious leader other than Jesus Christ. The answer was : " I can follow no leader who leads those who follow into the grave and who leaves them there. I can follow no leader who is held in the place of the dead. Jesus Christ led the way into the tomb, it is true, and therefore all who are not freed by translation from that experience will, perforce, have to follow Him into the grave also. *But He did not remain in the grave.* Death could not hold Him in the place of the dead. CHRIST AROSE, and led the way out from the tomb on the other side. Therefore we follow Him and follow Him alone, ' who only hath immortality.' His Gospel is demonstrated by His resurrection from the dead, and only His ; therefore we follow and rejoice in Him."

THE RESURRECTION FROM THE DEAD AS THE GREAT HOPE.

We shall have time but for one brief illustration of this. St. Peter had a vivid realisation of the economic status he and his associate disciples had reduced themselves to by following the Lord. Our Lord had declared, " foxes have holes and the birds of the air have nests, but the Son of Man has not where to lay His head." Peter therefore said unto Him, " Behold, we have forsaken all and have followed thee ; what shall we have, therefore ? "

THE RESURRECTION OF THE DEAD

It was a plain and a very reasonable question. The answer is just as plain, and we submit just as reasonable. But only so if we assume the veritable reality of the resurrection of the dead, and of the restoration of all things. This is the very obvious answer to the question of St. Peter : " And Jesus said unto them : Verily I say unto you, That ye which have followed me, *in the regeneration when the Son of Man shall sit in the throne of his glory,* ye also shall sit upon twelve thrones, judging the twelve tribes of Israel. And everyone that hath forsaken houses or brethren, or sisters, or father, or mother, or wife, or children, or lands, for my name's sake *shall receive an hundredfold,* and shall inherit everlasting life."

Mark, Our Lord's word is solemnly pledged to the disciples, and the writing under His hand which carries that pledge is recorded in the Scriptures. The security is therefore sure. It is better than Company Stocks, Railroad or Government Bonds, for it has a more sure backing and it carries on into the eternal state, or rather into the millennial period, which Government and Company Bonds do not. And the same security is offered to all who shall sacrifice for the Lord and His Kingdom, or who shall make investments therein.

An hundredfold is ten thousand per cent. This is the best guaranteed investment of which we have any knowledge. Foolish will be the person who does not invest therein.

The resurrection from the dead lies at the basis

of this great grant from the throne of the Lord, sealed with His own Name.

What a hope ; what a certainty is this for all who accept the Lord as Saviour and King.

THE PLACE OF THE RESURRECTION OF THE DEAD IN THE PROGRESS OF NATURAL PHENOMENA.

There was a time when the void, the supposedly infinite space where now swings the material universe, was empty of material things.

There came a day when in that space material things appeared. " In the beginning God created the heaven and the earth."

Up to a certain day the worlds of the Solar system had not been formed. In process of astronomical time the sun, moon, and planets took their places in the Solar system, and their motions were established in the heavens.

Up to a certain day there had been no appearance of life on the earth. There came a day when life appeared on the earth.

Up to a certain day or period there had been no conscious life. Then came a day when conscious life appeared.

Up to a later day there had not been a man upon the earth. Then came the day-dawn of the human period.

Up to a certain time man had lived unconscious of death. Then came a day when the first man passed through the gates of death.

Up to a certain morning of glorious memory no man had permanently returned from the grave.

Then came the Resurrection morning, when Our Lord burst the barriers of the tomb and arose triumphant over death.

Up to a certain day there had never a man ascended to heaven clad in his resurrection body. There came Ascension morning, when Christ ascended " and a cloud received Him out of their sight."

Until to-day the bodies of the generality of the dead rest sleeping in the grave. But there shall come a day when the " Dead in Christ shall arise first, and we who are alive and remain shall be changed " ; that is to say, translated.

Up to to-day no man who has ascended to God from the earth has ever returned to dwell again. But the day shall come when " He shall descend from heaven with a shout, with the voice of the archangel and the trump of God," and so coming, He shall bring His saints with Him.

Thus we see that in the progress of the great phenomena of nature, the resurrection of the dead has its place, and the day is not now far distant when the dead in Christ will arise at the sound of His voice, and the living in Christ with them will put on His likeness and go with Him into the millennial glory.

The personal glory of that time is thus contrasted with that of the life surrendered here, at death, or by translation at the coming of Our Lord :

So also is the resurrection of the dead. It is sown in corruption ; it is raised in incorruption :

It is sown in dishonour ; it is raised in glory ; it is sown in weakness ; it is raised in power :

It is sown a natural body ; it is raised a spiritual body. There is a natural body, and there is a spiritual body.

And so it is written, The first man Adam was made a living soul ; the last Adam was made a quickening spirit.

Howbeit that was not first which is spiritual, but that which is natural ; and afterward that which is spiritual.

The first man is of the earth, earthy ; the second man is the Lord from heaven.

As is the earthy, such are they also that are earthy ; and as is the heavenly, such are they also that are heavenly.

And as we have borne the image of the earthy, we shall also bear the image of the heavenly.

Now this I say, brethren, that flesh and blood cannot inherit the kingdom of God ; neither doth corruption inherit incorruption.

Behold, I show you a mystery : We shall not all sleep, but we shall all be changed.

In a moment, in the twinkling of an eye, at the last trump ; for the trumpet shall sound, and the dead shall be raised incorruptible, and we shall be changed.

For this corruptible must put on incorruption, and this mortal must put on immortality.

So when this corruptible shall have put on incorruption, and this mortal shall have put on immortality, then shall be brought to pass the saying that is written, Death is swallowed up in victory.

O death, where is thy sting ?   O grave, where is thy victory ?

The sting of death is sin ; and the strength of sin is the law.

But thanks be to God, which giveth us the victory through Our Lord Jesus Christ.

Therefore, my beloved brethren, be ye sted-fast, unmoveable, always abounding in the work of the Lord, forasmuch as ye know that your labour is not in vain in the Lord.

CHAPTER VI

Eternal Judgment

Note the following quotation: "The signification of the Hebrew word is much wider than that of the Greek 'krites,' the Latin 'judex,' or the English 'judge.' The judge was not only the vindicator, the punisher, but also the defender, the 'deliverer.'"—Int. Crit. Com.

In common English the word "judgment" is limited to the function of the British judge. He represents the King in the administration of justice. If there is a case *against the accused*, or *against the defendant*, the judge acts. If there be no case against such an one the judge dismisses the case. He punishes, he estimates and imposes damages. He does not deliver the injured except incidentally, and he does not reward virtue.

But the judge in the Bible sense of the term performs all the functions of the King: punishing crime, righting the wrong, delivering the oppressed, rewarding virtue. In fact, *to judge is to rule.*

With this Bible meaning of the term in mind let us now approach the last of this series of foundation doctrines, Eternal Judgment.

ETERNAL JUDGMENT

The Punitive Clauses of Eternal Judgment.

First we come to *the fact of* Sin.

" By one man sin entered into the world ; and death by sin."

This is a tremendous statement of Holy Writ. Human experience, carried to almost universal proportions, testifies to the fact that sin is in the world, and death by sin.

The illustration of this tragedy of history is given in the Jehovah Elohim (Lord God) section of the Creation story, which begins with the fourth verse of the second chapter of Genesis. In the process of that narrative we read " And the Lord God commanded the man . . ."

Up to that moment the will of man had been the law of his being. From that moment the expressed will of God became law to the man. At that moment began the prayer, later voiced by Our Lord, " Thy will be done on earth, as it is in heaven."

Up to that moment temptation for the man had been a psychical impossibility. True his mental standards had been exalted above that of other orders of life on earth, for he alone was created " in the likeness of God." But of moral standards, these had not as yet appeared. As we have said, the will of man was the law of his being, as the instinct of the lower orders is the law of their being. Not until the will of God became law to the man was there the possibility of temptation to refuse to do that will and to determine to follow his own will, which latter is the " another law in my

73

members " of which St. Paul speaks in his Epistle to the Romans.

Immediately upon the will of God being placed as a crown of glory upon the head of man, as the new law of his life and conduct, came the tempter and the temptation.

Then came sin ; judgment ; condemnation ; the death penalty ; coupled with the promise of the Redeemer, and the Atonement. " The seed of the woman shall bruise thy head. . ."

Thus was the first trial court of eternal judgment set on earth, and the first sentence delivered under it.

There came the enunciation of the law. "In the day that thou eatest thereof, thou shalt surely die." This is reiterated through the ages in the formula, " The soul that sinneth it shall die." And so death passed upon all men, for that all have sinned.

Now in the Divine procedure the status of the case seems to be this. The enemy, which is the Devil, seems to have thus reasoned : " Jehovah Elohim has just formed man of the dust of the earth and breathed into his nostrils the breath of life and man became a living soul. What is the purpose of this new formation ? What is to be the destiny of this new-formed creature ? Is it not that he should be prepared to occupy the place which I and my fellows have vacated through rebellion against the authority of Jehovah ?

Further, Jehovah Elohim has just endowed man with the glory of doing the will of God ; and thus of acting in a sphere far above that to which the man has been created. Thus manifesting the fact that he is to achieve a higher destiny than his beginnings would indicate.

But now comes my opportunity. If the man disobey the command of God he will offend against the law of eternal righteousness, and shall die. I will, therefore, secure his disobedience, and that will be to secure his destruction."

The fact of the success of the temptation is stated clearly.

But with the man, it would seem unexpectedly, the Devil came into judgment also, and a most unexpected judgment. The authority and power which " shall bruise thy head " because of this sin shall be " the seed of the woman " whom thou hast tempted to the fall of the race.

It would seem that even so this would be a triumph for the Devil against Jehovah. For the law cannot be altered even by the Divine will. *What it is, it is ; the eternal law of righteousness.* It would seem to the enemy that in order to save his creature from the consequence of his transgression, Jehovah would exercise His Divine sovereignty, and forgive the sinner. But this would be to break the eternal law of righteousness. It would be what our courts would call " compounding a felony," which is to be a partaker in the felony. And thus Jehovah Elohim would discredit the law.

But not so. " THAT HE MIGHT BE JUST, AND THE JUSTIFIER," Jesus Christ offered Himself, the sinless One, to take upon Himself the punishment of the sinner, and thus to restore him to sinless life again. Not as a sacrifice to God the Father, as many believe, but as an atonement under the eternal law of righteousness.

So, while man went his weary way under the burden of sin and death, the " Lamb of God was slain from the foundation of the world."

Then, " once in the end of the world Christ appeared to put away sin by the sacrifice of Himself," and the great act of the Atonement, *of such vital importance in the Court of Eternal Judgment*, took place, and has been accepted in heaven.

Now that great fact and act is offered to the sinner. He may take out his redemption, and through the blood of the everlasting Covenant be made clean ; or he may elect to remain under the condemnation of the eternal law.

Thus the Court of Eternal Judgment sits, and David thus sings of its administration :

" The judgments of the Lord are true and right- eous altogether. More to be desired are they than gold, yea than much fine gold ; sweeter also than honey and the honeycomb."

The judgments of the Lord are *true, righteous, valuable*, and *sweet*.

" Moreover, by them is thy servant warned ; and in keeping of them there is great reward."

UNIVERSALITY OF LAW.

God's entire universe is subject to law. This is true in *the " natural world."* It is subject utterly to natural law, such, for instance, as the law of gravitation. This is true in *the " psychical world."* There is a law governing our minds of which we are instinctively conscious, and to which we know ourselves to be subject. This is also true *in the spiritual world.* There is a spiritual law, of which God, in His character and attributes, is the expression and living embodiment. Under this law He says to us : " Be ye Holy, *for I am Holy."*

There is growing out of all this *a system of law* which is the expression of the eternal law of righteousness. That system is contained in the Commandments, Statutes and Judgments of Jehovah.

Here is the expression of the conclusion of that law : " The soul that sinneth, it shall die."

Here is the verdict under that law : " We have all sinned, and come short of the glory of God."

Here is the judgment : " All we like sheep have gone astray. We have turned every one to his own way ; and *the Lord hath laid on Him the iniquity of us all."*

Here is the delivery from THE CURSE OF THE LAW: " *Therefore being justified by faith, we have peace with God."*

Here is the assurance : " *There is therefore now no condemnation to them which are in Christ Jesus."*

" Christ hath redeemed us *from the curse of the law*, being made a curse for us : for it is written, Cursed is every one that hangeth on a tree."

Thus we see that, from the standpoint to which this theme makes its appeal to us, *there is a wide-*

open pathway for every soul to escape from the judgment imposing the curse of the law, which is death.

Let us see to it that our own individual case is cleared in the Divine Court, and that we have taken out the personal assurance of freedom from condemnation. This is a matter to which *every adult must give personal attention.* It cannot be obtained from man ; neither prelate, priest, nor layman. *It must be obtained by personal approach to Jesus Christ, the only Mediator.* The session of His court is always sitting. The door to His Presence is always open. The assurance of justification is always ready to be given, as a free gift of God, to the personal applicant who approaches the footstool of the Lord.

The place of approach is in our own heart. " When thou prayest, enter into thy closet ; and when thou hast shut thy door, pray to thy Father which is in secret ; and thy Father which seeth in secret shall reward thee openly." This is the instruction for our approach as given by Our Lord Himself.

This matter, of infinite import to us, having been attended to, let us go on to examine this foundation doctrine from the broader standpoint.

Eternal Judgment

Eternal. This word touches the infinite.

In the Court of Eternal Judgment, *the Atonement* for the sins of man, and *the Redemption* of the nation Israel, are well-established factors.

Whether the Incarnation and the Atonement

have wider scope than the earthly field of administration we have no knowledge. But as they are made to fit into the scheme of ETERNAL JUDGMENT it may well be so.

Whether the sacrificial ministry of Our Lord has a wider scope than earth or not, *it is certain that eternal judgment* has such a wider scope, embracing the whole of the universe as far as we have knowledge of it.

Nature in all its forms, and in all its expanse, answers to the will of Him who is described as " upholding all things by the word of His power." Into this we need not go further than to say that *all the activities of scientists from the very beginning have been based upon the assumption that all nature acts in obedience to, and in accordance with, established law.*

Our own human family reacts to a higher form of law than does any other earthly species of which we have knowledge. *Humanity reacts to the Divine will.* Of all the species of the earth, humanity is reserved to judgment in the way of trial, reward and punishment. The conviction of this is ingrained in the mentality of all but the very lowest types of men. Perhaps of all men.

But we read of other and higher orders of being.

The Demons are subject to law, and are conscious of the fact of broken law. They express dread of the consequences. For instance, the demons at Gadara said to Our Lord, " Art Thou come to torment us BEFORE THE TIME ? "

The Devils, a more powerful order of beings,

" are reserved in chains and darkness against the judgment of that great day." They are conscious of law and judgment, and have rebelled against both, awaiting the consequences in chains.

The Angels, which preserved their purity and passed up to serve before the throne of God ; the " angels which excel in strength, which do His commandments, hearkening unto the voice of His word," are conscious of law and judgment, and it is their delight to obey.

The judgment seat of The Eternal therefore embraces within the scope of its jurisdiction all these orders of life, and, we presume, all orders of life.

It is a universe of order, of law, of judgment.

Jehovah, the administrator of law, is a figure of ultimate Majesty, presented to us for our worship in the doctrine of eternal judgment.

SAVIOURSHIP.*

The word judgment also means *Saviourship*. " The Lord saved Israel by the hand of the judges " is a very common statement of the Old Testament histories. Regarding sinful man, it is a glorious thing to remember that *the Judge of all* is *the Saviour of all* who trust in Him.

Therefore, the doctrine of *eternal judgment* is also the doctrine of *eternal Saviourship*. What a " sweet " and " valuable " doctrine is this! Now as to the execution of judgment for us.

*The writer is indebted to Rev. Arthur Pritchard for this beautiful thought of the Judge-Saviour.

First, we consider the great ordinance of Calvary, where " Jesus Christ by the grace of God tasted death for every man."

There followed the presentation in "heaven itself" of the Blood of Our Lord, by Himself offered, in proof that the penalty attaching to the sins of men has been fully paid. Let us be glad and rejoice in the fact, and let us not be such proud and foolish ones as to put these glorious acts of Divine administration away. Let us remember that to put them away is to put our share in the facts away, and we thus stubbornly insist on standing out exposed to the consequences of rebellion, and to the sanctions of the law " in that case made and provided."

In the Kingly administration is *the gift of eternal life* to all those who are not too stubborn, or too proud, to accept the fact of the Atonement.

"THE PRINCE OF THIS WORLD IS JUDGED"

This is a major act of eternal judgment. Men have sinned and come short of the Glory of God. For such, an Atonement has been made. This, in part, *because they are victims of a wiser and more powerful agent in the physical, psychical and perhaps spiritual world,* namely, the Devil.

But the " Prince of this world " must answer for the rebellion of this world and for all the consequences which follow. " The Prince of this world is judged." And the judgment pronounced in the Garden is that his final overthrow shall come from the hand of " the seed of the woman," or rather from his heel—no angel hosts shall intervene. The glory of final victory now brought very near shall be to the " Son of Man," leading the hosts of the redeemed in final conflict with the Devil and all his forces. " And the Devil which deceived them was cast into the lake of fire."

Here is an act of Divine judgment in which all will agree. The author of sin, suffering, and death in the world, the Adamic world, must certainly be dealt with by eternal judgment, and we are given to see beforehand his judgment.

Eternal judgment must be also looked upon as embracing in its process the freeing of the race of Adam from sin and its accompanying disease and death, the consequences of the broken law. All this is covered by the teaching of the Church on the sanctification of the people of God.

Further, it must be looked upon as the completion of the work, undertaken when " the Lord God commanded the man," of *raising the race to that point where the will of God becomes both the law and the habit of life for the man.* This also is presented under the great law of regeneration.

Again, it must be looked upon as *the Divine activity in the restoration or regeneration of all things, including the physical and psychical worlds* which have been affected by the rebellion of man and of devils.

Eternal judgment must also be looked upon as *God's eternal rule in righteousness* over the new heaven and the new earth. This is set forth gloriously in the last two chapters of the Bible.

These chapters look beyond the Great White Throne day, which will be the last session of that court which deals with sin and death, to the Eternal Kingdom the capital of which is the Holy City, new Jerusalem, from which flows the river of life, and in which is the dwelling-place of God, in the midst of Israel His redeemed.

So we see the enthroned Judge, the King of Glory, carrying forward every branch of the Divine administration even to the ends of the universe and on into eternity.

His Judgment is true; His Saviourship is glorious; His Kingship is the sum of all perfection. It is our glory to have been justified from the charge of sin, by faith in God. It is our privilege to be fellow-labourers with Him in carrying forward the affairs of His jurisdiction, with Him to suppress the wrong, and to establish righteousness.

What a crowning glory is there in this last of the foundation doctrines, Eternal Judgment!

" Therefore, leaving the principles of the doctrine of Christ, let us go on unto perfection, not laying again the foundation. . . . And this will we do if God permit."

The Perfection to which we are called to " go on " we shall next consider.

CHAPTER VII

GOING ON UNTO PERFECTION

" THEREFORE leaving the principles of the doctrine of Christ, let us go on unto perfection ; not laying again the foundation of repentance from dead works, and of faith toward God,

" Of the doctrine of baptisms, and of laying-on of hands, and of resurrection of the dead, and of eternal judgment.

" And this will we do, if God permit." (Heb. vi, 1-3.)

We have dealt with the foundation doctrines, which we are now called upon to leave, in the preceding six chapters. They cover the ground of systematic theology.

The Church has been engaged in laying this foundation throughout all the Christian dispensation. Surely the foundation has been laid. Surely all that can be said has been said and written about the doctrines therein contained. It is time to go on with the building of the superstructure.

We must not *discard the foundation,* but we must " go on " with our building upon that foundation. It is not a call to march forward on the road. It is a call *to get on with the structure of the building.*

Many have become wearied with the constant foundation laying. None more so than the theological colleges connected with the Universities. It is well to be wearied with a task *when the task is done.* It is well to demand progress *when the first stage has been accomplished.*

Therefore we will essay to " go on unto perfection."

Let us examine the Great Architect's plans for the building, the foundation of which we have already examined.

Many, hearing or reading this exhortation, think instantly of developing on this foundation a perfect individual Christian character. This is a very desirable aim ; but it is not the teaching of this particular passage of Scripture. The passage refers to the establishment of a National Kingdom. Others would think of building upon such a foundation of Christian doctrine *a glorious Christian Church.* We look, however, in vain for a Cathedral or Church in the plans set forth for the building. The Church, as to doctrine and procedure, is contained in the six-coursed foundation.

The Great Architect's plans call for the erection upon the foundation of the Christian doctrines of *a Throne, Sceptre and Kingdom.* It is *a Royal Palace* instead of an ecclesiastical Temple here presented.

The Throne, Sceptre and Kingdom is on the earth, and the rule connected with it is an earthly rule, the subject of which is an earthly nation, i.e., the nation Israel.

In order that we may get the fulness of this great exhortation it will be necessary that we should take in somewhat of the nature and scope of the document in which it is contained, namely, the Epistle to the Hebrews.

The Epistle to the Hebrews is a most wonderful Epistle. *It is not an anonymous Epistle.*

The question is being asked again and again, " Who is the author of the Epistle to the Hebrews." The answers given to the question are various. Yet the Epistle seems to give its own answer to the question.

When receiving an epistle in these our days, one has to turn to the end to find the signature ; thus to determine the authorship of the letter which has come to us. In letters of the age in which the Epistle to the Hebrews was written it was not so. *The very first word of the Epistle was the signature of the author.* Thus the recipient of a letter was never left in doubt for a moment as to who his correspondent might be.

It is so with the letters of St. Paul, of St. Peter, and of the other Apostles. *The signature is the first word of the letter.*

The first word in the Epistle to the Hebrews is the name " GOD."

This, we are convinced, is not an accident. The human authorship is withheld by the influence of the Holy Spirit, *that the name " GOD " might appear in all its significance in the signature place in the Epistle.*

So we have come to regard this most wonderful Epistle as *a letter from the hand of our Heavenly Father Himself.* What a privilege to receive such a letter, in the signature place of which is the Name " GOD." Surely it is a letter from Heaven to us.

If this be the case, *what is the subject of the letter*? What could there be on this earth of ours of sufficient importance for our Heavenly Father to write to us, even through the pen of His chosen servant, whoever that may be?

The subject of the letter is

" HIS SON."

Surely this is a matter which the Father would delight to cause to be written, even as He caused His voice to be heard at the Baptism of Our Lord; and upon the " Holy Mount " of Trans-figuration, in testimony to " His Son."

The majestic form of words, and the infinite importance of the matter, are worthy even of Our Father which is in Heaven.

Let us follow the majesty of the opening sentences.

" God, who at sundry times and in divers manners spake in time past unto the fathers by the prophets,

1. Hath in these last days spoken unto us by his Son,
2. Whom he hath appointed heir of all things (Omega),
3. By whom also he made the worlds (Alpha);
4. Who being the brightness of his glory,
5. And the express image of his person,

6. And upholding all things by the word of his power,
7. When he had by himself purged our sins,
8. Sat down
9. On the right hand of the Majesty on high ;
10. Being made so much better than the angels, as he hath by inheritance obtained a more excellent name than they."

In this majestic form *the Son* is introduced to us.

The Epistle proceeds to show that He is better than the angels in a wonderful division of the Epistle. (Chapter i, 4-14 ; and ii, 1-9.)

" For unto which of the angels said he at any time, Thou art my Son, this day have I begotten thee ?   And again, I will be to him a Father, and he shall be to me a Son ? "   What a wonderfully expressive thing that question mark is!   It makes perfectly clear that herein there has been a word spoken to Our Lord to which the angels can never attain.   Other questions follow to the same purpose, namely, that God never spake thus to the angels.

" And again, when he bringeth in the firstbegotten into the world, he saith, And *let all the angels of God worship him.*

" And of the angels he saith, Who maketh his angels spirits, and his ministers a flame of fire."

Having thus made clear that angels are ministers, not sons ; created, not begotten ; He then as God, the enthroned Father, presents to our adoring eyes, God, the enthroned Son, thus :

" But unto the Son he saith, Thy *throne, O God,* is for ever and ever : a *sceptre* of righteousness is the *sceptre* of thy *kingdom* . . ."

Deity, throne, sceptre, kingdom—these are all included in this wonderful phrasing of introduction *by the enthroned and eternal Father of the enthroned and everlasting Son.*

Let us think for a moment. *This is language addressed to One who is incarnate, a Man who once dwelt on this earth of ours.* He was born in a village, the position of which is well known. He lived His life in another village equally well known. He travelled over roads still pressed by human feet. He visited the city of Jerusalem time and again, as many readers of this book have done. He was there apprehended, tried, declared innocent, yet delivered to His enemies, and by them was put to death.

He was buried in a tomb which still remains. He rose again from the dead, and ascended into Heaven. Seated there at the right hand of the Majesty on High, *He is the subject of this testimony of the Father.*

That wonderful testimony goes on : " Thou hast loved righteousness, and hated iniquity ; therefore God, even thy God, hath anointed thee with the oil of gladness above thy fellows."

This Divine anointing is the anointing of the King. It is well known to the House of David, the occupants of the throne of which are anointed with the holy oil as King. But this, the Everlasting Son of the Eternal Father, has been anointed with the oil of gladness above His fellows.

Again the Divine Voice proceeds : " And " (that is to say, this is an additional testimony, showing how infinitely above the angels is the Son), " And, Thou, Lord, in the beginning *hast laid the foundation of the earth: and the heavens are the works of thine hands* .

" They shall perish ; but thou remainest ; and they all shall wax old as doth a garment :

"And as a vesture shalt thou fold them up, and they shall be changed : but thou art the same, and thy years shall not fail.

" But to which of the angels said he at any time, Sit on my right hand, until I make thine enemies thy footstool ? " (The question mark again is there, and the expected answer which the reader will not fail to give is, Never.)

Yes, this Person is greater than the angels.

But this Person became incarnate. In so becoming He " was made a little lower than the angels—FOR—the suffering of death, crowned with glory and honour." (What glory, what honour ?) The answer comes swiftly : " That he by the grace of God—SHOULD—taste death for every man." This is the supreme glory, the supreme honour (see chap. ii, 9-18).

The wonderful testimony goes on to show that He is also greater than Moses, that He is greater than Levi and that He is greater than Abraham. Remember what this instruction would mean to the Hebrew mind of the day in which this Epistle was written. Greater than angels! Greater than Moses! Greater than Levi! Greater than Abraham! Then surely He was the greatest of the sons of men ; indeed, He is the Son of Man, as He is the Son of God.

THRONE, SCEPTRE, KINGDOM.

The activities of the Son contemporary with us are of the utmost importance, for on them depends our relationship to God. He is herein revealed to us as *the Son, possessed of throne, sceptre and kingdom.* Let us follow the Voice of the Father in this wonderful demonstration.

" Therefore leaving the principles of the doctrine of Christ, let us go on unto perfection ; . . . And this will we do, if God permit."

How shall we go on in this progress ? How shall we proceed with the building upon the sure foundation ? We must go back to God's unchanging plan, which commences for us in God's covenants and promises made to Abraham.

Chapter vi, 13-15 : " *For when God made promise to Abraham,* because he could swear by no greater, he sware by himself,

" Saying, Surely blessing I will bless thee, and multiplying I will multiply thee.

" And so, after he had patiently endured, he obtained the promise."

Now, why should this reference to Abraham and the promise made to him be thus thrust into the very forefront of the " going on " ? Why should the very first step of the post-foundation building be *the Abrahamic covenant,* especially as the study introduced to us in this most wonderful Epistle is a study of the Son of GOD ?

It is because of the evident fact that *Jesus Christ stepped into the very heart of the Abrahamic covenant, and that His throne, sceptre and kingdom are founded absolutely upon that covenant.*

It is also because of the fact that *the seal to that Abrahamic covenant is the blood of Our Lord Jesus Christ,* " once offered," as this wonderful Scripture goes on to show.

It was to Abraham that Melchisedec came, when first Abraham took upon him *the kingly function of making war for the liberation of the captive and for the scattering of predatory power.* Thus coming, Melchisedec " brought forth bread and wine," and ministered to Abraham the first recorded Sacrament of the Lord's Supper ; thus in anticipation showing forth that which in the same elements we commemorate, namely, " The Lord's death till He come." This was the seal to the Abrahamic covenant.

The voice which speaks these words goes on, in the discussion of the covenant made with Abraham (Heb. vi, 16-20) :

For men verily swear by the greater : and an oath for confirmation is to them an end of all strife.

Wherein God, willing more abundantly to shew unto the heirs of promise the immutability of his counsel, confirmed it by an oath :

That by two immutable things, in which it was impossible for God to lie, we might have a strong consolation, who have fled for refuge to lay hold upon the hope set before us :

Which hope we have as an anchor of the soul, both sure and stedfast, and which entereth into that within the veil ;

Whither the forerunner is for us entered, even Jesus, made an high priest for ever after the order of Melchisedec.

Therefore, by two " immutable things," namely, the *promise of* GOD and the *oath of* GOD, we may know that the promise once made to Abraham stands ; sealed by the blood of Jesus Christ, the " Magna Charta " of His priestly ministry.

CHAPTER VIII

GOING ON UNTO PERFECTION—(*contd.*)

WE continue our study of the foundation doctrines, and the " going on unto perfection," which we have carried on in the preceding seven chapters— " Which hope we have as an anchor of the soul, both sure and stedfast, and which entereth into that within the veil ; Whither the forerunner is for us entered, even Jesus, made an high priest for ever after the order of Melchisedec " (Heb. vi, 19, 20).

As we read this well-known passage we see with somewhat of surprise that the sure and steadfast anchor of the soul is the promise made and confirmed to Abraham ; and that it is in line with the fulfilment of the promise so made and confirmed that Jesus is for us entered within the veil.

It is in line with the same promises that He is made a Priest for ever after the order of Melchisedec.

If therefore we would understand the Priesthood of Jesus Christ, we should have before us the foundation promises so made, and confirmed to Abraham.

We quote certain passages which present the promises, and show that they refer to the elements which provide for the throne, sceptre and kingdom of Our Lord—i.e. peoples, nations, kings :

GOING ON UNTO PERFECTION

And when Abram was ninety years old and nine, the Lord appeared to Abram, and said unto him, I am the Almighty God ; walk before me, and be thou perfect.

And I will make my covenant between me and thee, and will multiply thee exceedingly.

And Abram fell on his face : and God talked with him, saying,

As for me, behold, my covenant is with thee, and thou shalt be a father of many nations.

Neither shall thy name any more be called Abram, but thy name shall be Abraham ; for a father of many nations have I made thee.

And I will make thee exceeding fruitful, and I will make nations of thee, and kings shall come out of thee.

And I will establish my covenant between me and thee and thy seed after thee in their generations for an everlasting covenant, to be a God unto thee, and to thy seed after thee.

And I will give unto thee, and to thy seed after thee, the land wherein thou art a stranger, all the land of Canaan, for an everlasting possession ; and I will be their God (Gen. xvii, 1-8).

And God said unto Abraham, As for Sarai thy wife, thou shalt not call her name Sarai, but Sarah shall her name be.

And I will bless her, and give thee a son also of her : yea, I will bless her, and she shall be a mother of nations ; kings of people shall be of her.

Then Abraham fell upon his face, and laughed, and said in his heart, Shall a child be born unto him that is an hundred years old? and shall Sarah, that is ninety years old, bear?

And Abraham said unto God, O that Ishmael might live before thee!

And God said, Sarah thy wife shall bear thee a son indeed; and thou shalt call his name Isaac: and I will establish my covenant with him for an everlasting covenant, and with his seed after him.

And as for Ishmael, I have heard thee: Behold, I have blessed him, and will make him fruitful, and will multiply him exceedingly; twelve princes shall he beget, and I will make him a great nation.

But my covenant will I establish with Isaac, which Sarah shall bear unto thee at this set time in the next year.

And he left off talking with him, and God went up from Abraham. (Gen. xvii, 15-22.)

And the angel of the Lord called unto Abraham out of the heaven the second time,

And said, By myself have I sworn, saith the Lord, for because thou hast done this thing, and hast not withheld thy son, thine only son:

That in blessing I will bless thee, and in multiplying I will multiply thy seed as the stars of the heaven, and as the sand which is upon the sea shore; and thy seed shall possess the gate of his enemies;

And in thy seed shall all the nations of the earth be blessed ; because thou hast obeyed my voice. (Gen. xxii, 15-18.)

The First Coming of Our Lord was in line with these promises and *the general promises* of the covenant, including a seed, nationhood, kingship ; redemption and atonement.

It is in connection with the same promises that He is now entered into " heaven itself " for us. It is in connection with the same promises that He shall come again to reign.

The Bible has made the priestly order of Aaron very familiar to us. But this wonderful Epistle to the Hebrews makes it quite clear that the Aaronic order of priests has been " taken away," and that the higher order of " Priests for ever after the order of Melchisedec " has taken its place. Let every priest or presbyter, whichever name is preferred for the same office, take note of this fact, Jesus has " taken away " the order of Aaron, that He might establish " the second," namely, the " Priest for ever after the order of Melchisedec " ; and *in the order of Melchisedec there is no succession.*

Let us be careful to distinguish between the " *Priests, the sons of Levi,*" and the " *Priests, the sons of Aaron.*" The Levitical priesthood, which is secular, remains. The Aaronic priesthood, which ministered alone at the altar, has been removed. There is still Levitical service, but there remaineth no more sacrifice for sin.

The following quotation shows that the Aaronic and Levitical priesthood is inferior to that of Melchisedec :

" *And without* all contradiction *the less* is blessed of *the better*. And here men that die receive tithes ; but there he receiveth them, of whom it is witnessed that he liveth.

" And as I may so say, *Levi also*, who receiveth tithes, PAYED TITHES IN ABRAHAM.

" For he was yet in the loins of his father, when Melchisedec met him.

" If therefore perfection were by the Levitical priesthood (for under it the people received the law), what further need was there that another priest should rise after the order of Melchisedec, and not be called after the order of Aaron.

" FOR THE PRIESTHOOD BEING CHANGED, THERE IS MADE OF NECESSITY A CHANGE ALSO OF THE LAW.

" For he of whom these things are spoken pertaineth to another tribe, OF WHICH NO MAN GAVE ATTENDANCE AT THE ALTAR.

" For it is evident that our Lord sprang out of Juda ; of which tribe Moses spake nothing concerning priesthood.

" And it is yet far more evident : for that after the similitude of Melchisedec there ariseth another priest

" Who is made, not after the law of a carnal commandment, but after the power of an endless life.

" For he testifieth, Thou art a priest for ever after the order of Melchisedec."

Let us now inquire what was the character of the priesthood of Melchisedec ?

" For this Melchisedec, king of Salem, priest of the most high God, who met Abraham returning from the slaughter of the kings, and blessed him ;

" To whom also Abraham gave a tenth part of all ; first being by interpretation

(1) King of righteousness, and after that also
(2) King of Salem, which is,
(3) King of peace ;
(4) Without father,
(5) Without mother,
(6) Without descent,
(7) Having neither beginning of days,
(8) Nor end of life ;
(9) but made like unto the Son of God ;
(10) abideth a priest continually."

The manifestation of the characteristics of Melchisedec here given is the manifestation of the characteristics of Jesus, " Who is made a priest for ever after the order of Melchisedec."

These specific manifestations are meaningless for us as far as the great and mysterious Melchisedec is concerned, but *they are instinct with life as far as Our Lord is concerned.*

Jesus is " without father." Not counting His descent from Joseph, who was the " husband of Mary," or any earthly father.

He is " without mother " ; from the time of His " entering into that which is within the veil," when He was made a Priest for ever. How

99

wonderfully that declaration places its finger upon and excludes the Mariolatry which has been intruded into His High Priestly work.

He was " without beginning of life." (" Very God of Very God.")

He is " without end of days." (" Who only hath immortality.")

But withal He is King! KING!! KING!!!

First being by interpretation King of Righteousness, and after that also " King of Salem, which is King of Peace."

Thus we see that the great Epistle sets forth the Person, Throne, Sceptre, and Kingdom of Jesus. His Priesthood is Royal, His administration is Kingly, His seat is not the Altar but the Throne, " on the right hand of the Majesty on High."

This is the reason why the priesthood should thus have been changed from the tribe of Levi and the house of Aaron to the tribe of Juda and the House of David. The latter is the sceptred tribe from which came the House of David, which is the Royal, Kingly, line.

Can we in our minds make the transfer of the High Priesthood of Jesus from the Temple to the Palace, from the Altar to the Throne?

But why should such a transfer be made?

The answer to that question is given most fully in the ninth chapter of this most wonderful Epistle. The Aaronic priest " STOOD, DAILY MINISTERING," IN THE TEMPLE, offering a constant succession of sacrifices, constantly pouring the blood, constantly slaying victims, and this throughout many generations.

But the ministry of Christ as *a sacrificing High Priest* is set forth in that chapter, from which we quote the following :

> For Christ is not entered into the holy places made with hands, which are the figures of the true ; but into heaven itself, now to appear in the presence of God for us :
>
> Nor yet that he should offer himself often, as the high priest entereth into the holy place every year with blood of others ;
>
> For then must he often have suffered since the foundation of the world : but now once in the end of the world hath he appeared to put away sin by the sacrifice of himself.
>
> And as it is appointed unto men once to die, but after this the judgment :
>
> So Christ was once offered to bear the sins of many : and unto them that look for him shall he appear the second time without sin unto salvation.   (Heb. ix, 24-28.)

The work of *the sacrificing Priesthood* of Jesus was FINISHED immediately upon His entering into Heaven itself.   In regard to that sacrificing Priesthood it is stated : " When he had by himself purged our sins, SAT DOWN on the right hand of the Majesty on high." Contrast this seated position with the Aaronic ministry, " STANDING, DAILY MINISTERING, in the Temple."

This is the FINISHED WORK OF CHRIST.

There remains the Kingly work of Christ.

Speaking of Himself, He declared " A certain nobleman went into a far country, to receive for himself a kingdom and to return." When He thus spoke, His hearers would have in memory the going to the far country, Italy, of Herod and other kings and governors, that they might receive for themselves this or that kingdom or office. The saying would be luminous to their minds in view of this illustration from contemporary life. " A certain nobleman went into a far country, to receive for himself a kingdom and to return." In this case the far country was " Heaven itself," and the nobleman, Jesus.

Thus He, having finished the work of His humiliation, went " into Heaven itself," first to present His own blood ONCE OFFERED ; then to *sit down* on the right hand of the Majesty on High, as far as sacrificial work is concerned, for " there remaineth no more sacrifice for sins," but also *to take up the activities of His Kingly Priesthood.*

It is manifest therefore that Our Lord's present Priesthood is that of King, King, King : after the order of Melchisedec.

First King of Righteousness. " A sceptre of righteousness is the sceptre of thy Kingdom."

1. He causes His people to be accounted righteous by virtue of the Atonement worked out by Himself at such a cost upon the Mount of Sacrifice. He causes His Nation Israel to be accounted righteous by virtue of the Redemption worked out by Himself at such a cost upon the

Hill of Calvary. This is an interim measure while His Grace is carrying forward the perfecting of His ministry. This is a legal process which secures our justification in the court of eternal righteousness—a most vital matter to each of us.

2. He constrains His people individually, and His nation as His nation, to act righteously by the restrictions of His law, and by His Kingly authority. His voice rings out in the words of the Decalogue, " Thou shalt not . . . Thou shalt not . . . Thou shalt not . . ." This is an interim process, necessary until His people in fulfilment of His promise become " all righteous," and find the Law of God written compellingly in their hearts. Thus He administers righteousness by the command to avoid evil.

3. He causes His people, and His nation, *to become righteous* by His sanctifying Grace. This is a process which is being pushed forward by the agency of the Holy Spirit, and the promise is that ultimately it shall reach absolute fulfilment, when every person, and every detail of every person's life, shall be " HOLINESS TO THE LORD."

He secures righteousness for sinful men through His atoning ministry. *He secures righteousness* for Israel, His sinful nation, by His redemption of Israel upon Calvary. He dispenses righteousness to the penitent, both individual and nation, when they call upon Him.

But upon those who reject the Redemption as a nation, and the Atonement as an individual, there is nothing " but a certain fearful looking for of judgment and fiery indignation which shall devour the adversaries."

" He that despised Moses' law died without mercy under two or three witnesses :

" Of how much sorer punishment judge ye, shall he be thought worthy, who hath trodden under foot the Son of God, and hath counted the blood of the covenant, wherewith he was sanctified an unholy thing, and hath done despite unto the spirit of grace ? "

Dispensing mercy to the penitent, individual and national ; and carrying out the justice of God to the impenitent, individual and national ; *He is the King of Righteousness.*

He reigns upon His Throne. He administers justice in that Court wherein is administered the eternal law of righteousness, not only to Israel, His nation, but also to the " All nations " which shall stand before the " Throne of His Glory," and not only to these, but also to the " Angels which kept not their first estate " ; who also made themselves terribly responsible for the seduction of angelic hosts in Heaven, and of the sons of Adam on earth. " When the Son of Man shall come in his glory, and all the holy angels with him, then shall he sit upon the throne of His Glory." This gives to us a flashing glimpse of Himself as the King of Righteousness.

As we proceed with this study we shall see that while His righteousness is enthroned in the heavens, it also acts in administering vigour for the widow and the fatherless on the earth.

GOING ON UNTO PERFECTION

He is also King of Salem.

But Salem is a geographical place on the earth.
It is a geographical point well-known. Many of
the readers of this article will have been there.
It is of small import to us where on the earth
Salem lies. *It is infinitely important for us to
realise that being King of Salem He is King in
this very earth, which is our dwelling-place.* " His
feet shall stand in that day upon the Mount of
Olives." Thus, while we have an anchor which
enters into that within the veil, the ship of the
Kingdom still rides the restless seas of this earth.
Once again, at midnight, He will rejoin the ship,
" walking on the waters."

This is an all-important thing. He is King in
Heaven. He is seated on the right hand of the
Majesty on High. But He is King of Salem on
the earth. Salem was *the capital of God's Kingdom
on earth,* is now officially the capital in another
location, and shall be restored to Jerusalem again
in due time. The High Priesthood of Jesus
includes the Kingship of Salem. For the present,
" Salem," or Jerusalem, is removed from its
geographical place. In view of this fact, the
promise is " Jerusalem *shall be inhabited again in
its own place, even in Jerusalem.*"

At present Jerusalem is the Capital of God's
people, Israel-Britain, and it is at the WEST-
MINSTER. Jerusalem, having the Temple therein,
was the Eastminster. But the Eastminster was
destroyed, and the Capital was removed to the
Westminster. By and by, " Salem," the official

Capital, shall go home again to its former geographical position, viz., Jerusalem. Wherever " Salem," the Capital of God's Kingdom, is *Jesus is there*, " *King of Salem.*"

" *Which is King of Peace.*"

What wonderful influences for peace go forth from that " Salem " which is at this time the Capital of the Kingdom. That influence is the " Pax Britannica." That is to say, " The Peace of the Covenant." We should even come more closely to literal translation by saying the " peace of the ships of the Covenant." Surely there never has been such an agent of peace on the earth as the " Salem " Throne ; the " BRITH (Covenant) ISH " (man) Throne, and of the Brith Annia (Covenant ships), and the Royal Navy which supports that Throne.

He is, then, King of *Righteousness*, King of *Salem*, King of *Peace*.

But the conditions of that peace are clearly set forth. It is not international. Being King, not yet over all the earth, but of " Salem " in the earth, it is not yet in His jurisdiction to command international peace. His peace is internal to His Kingdom, and is thus set forth by Isaiah in his message to the House of David.

For every battle of the warrior is with confused noise, and garments rolled in blood ; but this shall be with burning and fuel of fire.

For unto us a child is born, unto us a son is given : and the government shall be upon his shoulder : and his name shall be called Wonder-ful, Counsellor, The mighty God, The ever-lasting Father, The Prince of Peace.

OF THE INCREASE OF HIS GOVERNMENT AND PEACE THERE SHALL BE NO END, UPON THE THRONE OF DAVID, AND UPON HIS KINGDOM, TO ORDER IT, AND TO ESTABLISH IT WITH JUDG-MENT AND WITH JUSTICE FROM HENCEFORTH EVEN FOR EVER. THE ZEAL OF THE LORD OF HOSTS WILL PERFORM THIS. (Isa. ix, 5-7).

CHAPTER IX

The Field of Our Lord's Ministry

WE have been following the exhortation: "Therefore leaving the principles of the doctrine of Christ, let us go on unto perfection." We have seen that this exhortation is to go on to the knowledge of the High Priest by Kingship of Christ.

He is " a Priest for ever after the order of Melchisedec." Melchisedec is " Priest of the most high God."

" Without father, without mother, without descent, having neither beginning of days, nor end of life, but made like unto the Son of God ; abideth a priest continually."

All this is of mysterious import to us as far as Melchisedec is concerned. But the discussion we are reading in the most wonderful Epistle is not primarily regarding Melchisedec, but *is regarding Jesus Christ.*

The list of characteristics given above is presented as an illustration of that which Christ is as a " Priest for ever after the order of Melchisedec."

Of Jesus Christ, therefore, we must read :

Without father—(" I proceeded forth and came from God.")

Without mother—Who said to His mother, " Woman what have I to do with thee." In bearing the Christ child for the world, the Blessed Virgin Mary received honour above all other women. Having born the Son of man, she may have no further part in His Ministry. " Without mother." Therefore the introduction of the mother of Jesus into the Priestly Ministry is utterly forbidden.

Without descent—There are no succeeding generations in the Priesthood of Christ.

" He abideth a Priest for ever after the order of Melchisedec." There is no successorship in the Priesthood of Jesus Christ in that order.

Having neither beginning of life nor end of days, " Who only hath immortality,"

Melchisedec is three times King. Such also is the Priesthood of Jesus.

He is King of righteousness ;
King of Salem ;
King of Peace.

His Priesthood is Royal. He ministers, not at the altar, but on the throne. The testimony of the Father in this most wonderful Epistle is to *His Godhead, His throne, His sceptre*, and *His Kingdom.*

All these things we have seen at length in the two last chapters, but for the sake of our readers we recapitulate to this extent.

We now follow the instruction as to *the field of the Royal Ministry of our Lord.*

We must bring our thought *down from heaven* to the earth. We must extend our thought beyond the arena of the Church, as the exclusive field of His ministry, to that of the nation.

We must " go on " from doctrines, such as the foundation ones which we have already considered, to *national charters and covenants; national commandments and laws.* For, as we shall see, these are the matters with which His Kingly ministry is occupied.

" Now of the things which we have spoken this is the sum :

WE HAVE SUCH AN HIGH PRIEST,

who is set on the right hand of the throne of the Majesty in the heavens ;

A minister of the sanctuary, and of the true tabernacle, which the Lord pitched and not man.

For every high priest is ordained to offer gifts and sacrifices wherefore it is of necessity that this man have somewhat to offer.

FOR IF HE WERE ON EARTH HE SHOULD NOT
BE A PRIEST,

seeing that there are priests that offer gifts according to the law, who serve unto THE EXAMPLE AND SHADOW of heavenly things, as Moses was admonished of God when he was about to make the tabernacle : for, see, saith He, that thou make all things according to the pattern shewed to thee in the mount."

" But now hath he obtained a more excellent ministry, by how much also he is the mediator of a better covenant, which was established upon better promises."

" *A more excellent ministry,*"

" The mediator of a *better covenant,*"

" Established upon *better promises.*"

These things are very important, as will be manifest to all.

" For if the first covenant had been faultless, then should no place have been sought for the second."

For finding fault with them He saith, " Behold the days come, saith the Lord, when I will make a new covenant. . . . In that He saith, A new covenant, He hath made the first old. Now that which decayeth and waxeth old is ready to vanish away."

It will be important for us to see what is the covenant that is here set aside. *It is the national covenant* made with the nation Israel when they emerged from Egypt and were organised into God's Kingdom nation. This is most clearly stated in the text of the scripture we are studying, also in the eighth chapter of Hebrews, thus, " Not according to the covenant that I made with their fathers in the day when I took them by the hand to lead them out of the land of Egypt, because they continued not in my covenant, and I regarded them not," saith the Lord. The covenant thus removed had nothing to do with the unconditional covenants made with Abraham, Isaac and Jacob ; nor with the covenant later made with the House of David.

Where is the " first covenant " thus removed to be found ?

It will be found in the twenty-sixth chapter of Leviticus.

That covenant had two columns, one the " If " and the other the " but " column. " If " ye obey I will bless you—" but," if ye rebel I will punish you with a series of "seven times" punishment ; each seven times being two thousand five hundred and twenty years. The series to be imposed in succession, and to run concurrently when once they were imposed, until the time of their fulfil-ment, when they should end in succession as they began. The first imposed ending first, and so on.

Please read carefully the chapter named as part of this article, i.e. Lev. xxvi (26).

It is historic that Israel rebelled more and more until the punishment clauses of this covenant were imposed. These were imposed at the time of the captivities, and the punishment consisted in the captivities and wanderings during the periods named. Three out of the four sentences have now expired, and the last will expire by elapse of time not later than A.D. 1934-36.

On the expiry of the " old " covenant, Israel-Britain comes under the clauses of the " better covenant " founded upon " better promises."

In the new covenant there are no punishment clauses.

In it there is neither " If " nor " but."

It is not contingent on obedience, but it is founded upon the " I will," and the " They shall," of the Lord ; that is to say, it is founded upon *Divine Sovereign Grace.*

Let us ask ; who are the parties to the new covenant?

Jehovah is the " party of the first part."

The House of Israel is " the party of the second part."

What is the date of the new covenant?

" After those days, saith the Lord."

What are the days thus indicated?

Undoubtedly they are *the days of punishment under the first covenant*; which days stretched over the weary ages of twenty-five hundred and twenty years. The sentences were at all times subject to reversal upon Israel's repentance, which repentance, alas, never came.

What is the nature of the new covenant, the " better covenant established upon better promises " of which Christ has the " more excellent ministry "?

Clause I is as follows : It consists of a preamble, and three clauses. The preamble is as follows :

Heb. viii, 8-9.

For finding fault with them, he saith, Behold, the days come, saith the Lord, when I will make a new covenant with the house of Israel and with the house of Judah :

Not according to the covenant that I made with their fathers in the day when I took them by the hand to lead them out of the land of Egypt ; because they continued not in my covenant, and I regarded them not, saith the Lord.

Heb. viii. 10-12.

For this *is* the covenant that I will make with the house of Israel after those days, saith the Lord : I will put my laws in their mind, and write them in their hearts : and I will be to them a God, and they shall be to me a people :

And they shall not teach every man his neighbour, and every man his brother, saying, Know the Lord : for all shall know me, from the least to the greatest.

For I will be merciful to their unrighteousness, and their sins and their iniquities will I remember no more.

For the remainder of the clauses we must go to the original document from which the preamble and Clause I are here quoted. This quotation is enough to identify the document beyond question. We shall find the full document in Jer. xxxi. It reads as follows, the sub-headings being supplied by us, interlined :

(Preamble.)

Jer. xxxi. 31-34.

Behold, the days come, saith the LORD, that I will make a new covenant with the house of Israel, and with the house of Judah.

Not according to the covenant that I made with their fathers in the day *that* I took them by the hand to bring them out of the land of Egypt : which my covenant they brake, although I was an husband unto them, saith the LORD :

(Clause I.)   Restoration of the Law.

But this *shall be* the covenant that I will make with the house of Israel ; After those days, saith the LORD, I will put my law in their inward parts, and write it in their hearts ; and will be their God, and they shall be my people.

And they shall teach no more every man his neighbour, and every man his brother, saying, Know the LORD : for they shall all know me, from the least of them unto the greatest of them, saith the LORD ; for I will forgive their iniquity, and I will remember their sin no more.

(Clause II.)   The perpetuation of the nation.

Jer. xxxi, 35-37.

Thus saith the LORD, which giveth the sun for a light by day, *and* the ordinances of the moon and of the stars for a light by night, which divideth the sea when the waves thereof roar ; The LORD of hosts *is* his name :

If those ordinances depart from before me, saith the LORD, *then* the seed of Israel also shall cease from being a nation before me for ever.

Thus saith the LORD ; If heaven above can be measured, and the foundations of the earth searched out beneath, I will also cast off all the seed of Israel for all that they have done, saith the LORD.

(Clause III.)　The restoration of Jerusalem (Salem).

Jer. xxxi, 38-40.

Behold, the days come, saith the LORD, that the city shall be built to the LORD from the tower of Hananeel unto the gate of the corner.

And the measuring line shall yet go forth over against it upon the hill Gareb, and shall compass about to Goath.

And the whole valley of the dead bodies, and of the ashes, and all the fields unto the brook of Kidron, unto the corner of the horse gate toward the east, *shall be* holy unto the LORD ; it shall not be plucked up, nor thrown down any more for ever.

This covenant is made *with the House of Israel* as distinct from all other nations, even as distinct from the House of Judah. To the House of Judah shall be also a new covenant ; but it is not set forth, only promised, in this document, as good reason is ; for this covenant is with the House of Israel only.

That House is the Party of the second part to this covenant.

The covenant is to come into effect " After those days."

The covenant is based upon the sovereign grace of God, and not upon the contingency of Israel's obedience.　" I will," " They shall."

Let us now glance at the meaning of the clauses. Clause I deals with *the restitution of the Divine law in the House of Israel.* In the old covenant the law was *an external thing*, written upon external tables of stone. Under the new covenant it is *an internal thing* " written upon the fleshly tables of the heart."

Clause II deals with *the everlasting perpetuation of the nation Israel.* Let every student of the Word and Will of the Lord take careful notice here, and let every student and teacher beware of confusing this covenant with the House of Israel with Judah, for Judah is not included as all may see.

The nation Israel is infinitely more secure under the new covenant than under the old.

Under the old, Moses and his successors were the Ministers. Under the new, the more excellent ministry is that of Christ.

The old covenant was contingent upon Israel's obedience. In the new covenant there is no such contingency.

Under the old covenant it was a matter of *future* Redemption. Under the new covenant *the Redemption is complete*, and the new covenant *is sealed with the blood of Jesus Christ.*

Under the new covenant *the nation is established for ever*, under the oath of Jehovah. Therefore we must see in Israel the perpetual nation, *more of a New Testament fact than an Old Testament one;* a fact most clearly set forth in both. This is important.

Moreover, we see in that perpetual nation the

field of the exercise of the Royal functions of Our Lord.

Clause III deals with the city Jerusalem, or Salem, of which Jesus, " made a priest for ever after the order of Melchisedec," is King.

Official Jerusalem, as we see indicated in the twelfth chapter of Zechariah, for instance, has been established away from the geographical position of Jerusalem. Zechariah says, " Jerusalem shall be inhabited again in its own place even in Jerusalem," that is to say, official Jerusalem shall return to geographical Jerusalem.

In the same way official Zion is established away from the Hill of Zion. Isaiah records the promise, " My watchman shall see eye to eye when I bring again Zion." One cannot " bring again " that which has not been taken away.

The last clause of the new covenant promises *the restoration and enlargement of Jerusalem " after those days," " built to Jehovah."*

The last Clause III promises *the transformation of the " valley of the ashes and dead bodies "* into a garden. That is to say, it promises *the banishment of the fires of Gehennah, that age-long symbol, from the city of Jerusalem.* A most momentous illustration, which is included in the new covenant.

Those who have been watching the developments of the Holy Land will know that the improvements here stated are now well under way, not now to " Allah," but " to Jehovah."

This clause regarding Jerusalem is by way of *dating the new covenant,* the date is measured

according to *the experience of the City Jerusalem*—
" Blindness is happened unto Israel until . . ."

" *Jerusalem shall be trodden down* of the Gentiles *until* . . ." Jerusalem should be relieved from being trodden down by an alien people, dominated by an alien faith ; " Behold the days come, saith the Lord, that the city shall be built to the Lord . . ." " After these days."

All these matters matured in 1917 when Allenby entered, and the city ceased to be trodden down of the Gentiles, being set free in the name of Jehovah, the God and King of Israel. It was so set free by Allenby, at the head of the Israel-British armies.

This nation, including this city of " Salem," is the field of the Kingly Ministry of our Lord, as we must see by the study of this wonderful document of the new covenant.

CHAPTER X.

The March of the Covenant Bearers

WE have seen in the preceding chapters the national side of the New Covenant. In connection with this our Lord hath " obtained a more excellent ministry . . . he is the mediator of a better covenant which was established upon better promises . . ."

We have seen that He is : " A priest for ever after the order of Melchisedec,

King . . . of righteousness ;

King . . . of Salem ;

King . . . of Peace :

and that *Kingly administration* is the function of His High Priesthood, unlike that of the priesthood of the Aaron.

Let us now follow the statement and see that *there are ordinances of worship* connected with that Kingly Ministry of Jesus, and wherein they differ from the Mosaic ordinances. The tabernacle of the first covenant. We shall avoid our own presentation of this all-important theme, and let the Word speak for itself.

(Heb. ix, 1-10.)

1. " Then verily the first covenant had also ordinances of divine service, and a worldly sanctuary.

2. For there was a tabernacle made ; the first, wherein was the candlestick, and the table, and the shewbread ; which is called the sanctuary.

3. And after the second veil, the tabernacle which is called the Holiest of all ;

4. Which had the golden censer, and the ark of the covenant overlaid round about with gold, wherein was the golden pot that had manna, and Aaron's rod that budded, and the tables of the covenant ;

5. And over it the cherubims of glory shadowing the mercy seat ; of which we cannot now speak particularly.

6. Now when these things were thus ordained, the priests went always into the first tabernacle, accomplishing the service of God.

7. But into the second went the high priest alone once every year, not without blood, which he offered for himself, and for the errors of the people ;

8. The Holy Ghost this signifying, that the way into the holiest of all was not yet made manifest, while as the first tabernacle was yet standing :

9. Which was a figure for the time then present, in which were offered both gifts and sacrifices, that could not make him that did the service perfect, as pertaining to the conscience ;

10. Which stood only in meats and drinks, and divers washings, and carnal ordinances, imposed on them until the time of reformation."

The more perfect tabernacle of the New Covenant.

THE STATESMANSHIP OF JESUS

(Heb. ix, 11-14.)

11. " But Christ being come an high priest of good things to come, by a greater and more perfect tabernacle, not made with hands, that is to say, not of this building ;

12. Neither by the blood of goats and calves, but by his own blood he entered in once into the holy place, having obtained eternal redemption for us.

13. For if the blood of bulls and of goats, and the ashes of an heifer sprinkling the unclean, sanctifieth to the purifying of the flesh :

14. How much more shall the blood of Christ, who through the eternal Spirit offered himself without spot to God, purge your conscience from dead works to serve the living God ? "

Mediator of the New Testament.

(Heb. ix, 15-17.)

15. " And for this cause he is the mediator of the new testament, that by means of death, for the redemption of the transgressions that were under the first testament, they which are called might receive the promise of eternal inheritance.

16. For where a testament is, there must also of necessity be the death of the testator.

17. For a testament is of force after men are dead : otherwise it is of no strength at all while the testator liveth."

Dedicated with blood.

(Heb. ix, 18-28.)

18. " Whereupon neither the first testament was dedicated without blood.

19. For when Moses had spoken every precept to all the people according to the law, he took the blood of calves and of goats, with water, and scarlet wool, and hyssop, and sprinkled both the book, and all the people,

20. Saying, This is the blood of the testament which God hath enjoined unto you.

21. Moreover he sprinkled with blood both the tabernacle, and all the vessels of the ministry.

22. And almost all things are by the law purged with blood ; and without shedding of blood is no remission.

23. It was therefore necessary that the patterns of things in the heavens should be purified with these ; but the heavenly things themselves with better sacrifices than these.

24. For Christ is not entered into the holy places made with hands, which are the figures of the true ; but into heaven itself, now to appear in the presence of God for us :

25. Nor yet that he should offer himself often, as the high priest entereth into the holy place every year with blood of others ;

26. For then must he often have suffered since the foundation of the world : but now once in the end of the world hath he appeared to put away sin by the sacrifice of himself.

27. And as it is appointed unto men once to die, but after this the judgment :

28. So Christ was once offered to bear the sins of many ; and unto them that look for him shall he appear the second time without sin unto salvation."

The law a shadow of good things to come.

(Heb. x, 1-4.)

1. " For the law having a shadow of good things to come, and not the very image of the things, can never with those sacrifices which they offered year by year continually make the comers thereunto perfect.

2. For then would they not have ceased to be offered ? because that the worshippers once purged should have had no more conscience of sins.

3. But in those sacrifices there is a remembrance again made of sins every year.

4. For it is not possible that the blood of bulls and of goats should take away sins."

Christ recognised that " Sacrifices and offerings thou wouldest not."

(Heb. x, 5-6.)

5. " Wherefore when he cometh into the world, he saith, Sacrifice and offering thou wouldest not, but a body hath thou prepared me :

6. In burnt offerings and sacrifices for sin thou hast had no pleasure."

Christ the perfect offering.

In verse 5 He calls attention to the fact " a body hast thou prepared me." That body which should be the perfect and the final offering.

(Heb. x, 7-10.)

7. " Then said I, Lo, I come (in the volume of the book it is written of me) to do thy will,O God.

8. Above when he said, Sacrifice and offering and burnt offerings and offering for sin thou wouldest not, neither hadst pleasure therein ; which are offered by the law ;

9. Then said he, Lo, I come to do thy will, O God. He taketh away the first, that he may establish the second.

10. By the which will we are sanctified through the offering of the body of Jesus Christ once for all."

The " *daily ministering* " and " *offering ofttimes* " of the Aaronic priesthood.

(Heb. x, 11.)

11. And every priest standeth daily ministering and offering oftentimes the same sacrifices, which can never take away sins :

" *This man . . . offered one sacrifice for sins for ever.*"

(Heb. x, 12-14.)

12. " But this man, after he had offered one sacrifice for sins for ever, sat down on the right hand of God ;

13. From henceforth expecting till his enemies be made his footstool.

14. For by one offering he hath perfected for ever them that are sanctified."

The witness of the Holy Ghost to us,

(Heb. x, 15-25.)

15. " Whereof the Holy Ghost also is a witness to us : for after that he said before,

16. This is the covenant that I will make with them after those days, saith the Lord, I will put my laws into their hearts, and in their minds will I write them ;

17. And their sins and iniquities will I remember no more.

18. Now where remission of these is, there is no more offering for sin.

19. Having therefore, brethren, boldness to enter into the holiest by the blood of Jesus,

20. By a new and living way, which he hath consecrated for us, through the veil, that is to say, his flesh ;

21. And having an high priest over the house of God ;

22. Let us draw near with a true heart in full assurance of faith, having our hearts sprinkled from an evil conscience, and our bodies washed with pure water.

23. Let us hold fast the profession of our faith without wavering ; (for he is faithful that promised) ;

24. And let us consider one another to provoke unto love and to good works :

25. Not forsaking the assembling of ourselves together, as the manner of some is ; but exhorting one another : and so much the more, as ye see the day approaching."

What a wonderful presentation is this. How clear that *the sacrificing priesthood of Aaron has been set aside for ever;* and that *the sacrificing activity of our Lord has been finished for ever.*

How solemn the warning against the turning away from the great sacrifice to a new series of man-offered sacrifices for sins, which will have no recognition in heaven : but which on the contrary will bring down upon the head of the recalcitrant, " Fiery indignation."

(Heb. x, 26-27.)

26. "For if we sin wilfully after that we have received the knowledge of the truth, there remaineth no more sacrifice for sins,

27. But a certain fearful looking for of judgment and fiery indignation, which shall devour the adversaries."

Now follows a warning against despising the great doctrine and fact of the Atonement, to which we shall do well to give heed.

(Heb. x, 28-31.)

28. " He that despised Moses' law died without mercy under two or three witnesses :

29. Of how much sorer punishment, suppose ye, shall he be thought worthy, who hath trodden under foot the Son of God, and hath counted the blood of the covenant, wherewith he was sanctified, an unholy thing, and hath done despite unto the Spirit of grace ?

30. For we know him that hath said, Vengeance belongeth unto me, I will recompense, saith the Lord. And again, The Lord shall judge his people.

31. It is a fearful thing to fall into the hands of the living God."

CHAPTER XI

Mileposts on the Way

In our study of the Epistle which bears in the signature place the name GOD, that is to say, the Epistle to the Hebrews, we have dealt with the foundation doctrines of the Christian faith, namely, repentance from dead works, faith towards God, Baptisms, the laying-on of hands, the resurrection of the dead, and eternal Judgment.

We have also taken the next forward and seen that it is God's revealed plan that upon that foundation shall be built the Royal Palace, containing the throne and sceptre of the Lord, established over His Kingdom, Israel.

We have seen that the function of our Lord in His office as " the High Priest of our profession," He being " made a Priest for ever after the order of Melchisedec," is to administer the New Covenant, made with the House of Israel.

That administration consists of three lines of action.

I. The restoration of the Divine law in the House of Israel ; by writing it in the hearts of the Israel people.

II. The preservation of the nation Israel, made up of the seed of Abraham, Isaac, and Jacob, forever.

III. The restoration of the City of " Salem " and its final development to the name of Jehovah.

This is the primary course of our Lord's administration.

We have seen the " ordinances of Divine service " connected therewith, and that *the sacrificial work of our Lord and of all the order of Melchisedec* IS FINISHED. In connection with that order there never was, and never will be, more than one sacrifice ; that of our Lord ; and that *once offered*, only. Having made that sacrifice " Once for all " He is " sat down at the right hand of the Majesty on high."

" There remaineth no more sacrifice for sin."

God's one purpose and mission in the earth is to carry through this great national plan ; and through that national plan to carry through the Saviourship of the world. It has pleased God to make *the Son of Man the Saviour of the world.* It has also pleased God *to associate the seed of Abraham, Isaac, and Jacob with Him in that great Mission to humanity.*

This great work includes the *development of the Kingdom of God* on the earth, or " Of the increase of His government and peace there shall be no end, upon the throne of David and upon His Kingdom to order it and to establish it, with judgment and with justice, henceforth even for ever. The zeal of the LORD of Hosts shall accomplish this."

For this purpose *the nation Israel was established* that it might function as " His Dominion." For this cause it was separated from Judah, the sister nation. For this cause it was *Redeemed as a nation.* For should the nation fail, the cause would not succeed. For this purpose *it was established in " the Isles,"* and caused to become *" A nation and a company of nations, and a great people."*

But the plan also took in the *ecclesiastical side. A great national church was as requisite as a great nation* for the carrying out of the Divine purpose. Therefore was the " Church in the wilderness " established. For this cause the Aaronic priesthood was ordained. For this cause the tabernacle was built, and its ordinances given. For this cause Juda " my sanctuary " was separated from Israel, and " to them were committed the oracles of God." For this cause the Christian ministry was ordained, and the Christian Church organised, of which Jesus Christ is " the Apostle and High Priest."

Thus down through the ages the great plan has been progressing, and to-day it is reaching the end of a very important stage. " Upon us, now living, the end of the age has come," and we are moving towards the world-wide manifestation of the Kingdom and the Church of Christ, each of which is based upon Israel, and the head and centre of each of which is to-day in Great Britain.

The whole plan has been carried forward through the ages as far as the human side is concerned, by men of faith. It still must be so carried forward. Men of " knowledge " have claimed the right to possess the leadership of the movement. But they must fail. For there are many elements in the great plan, which plan is Divine, transcending human knowledge, although not contrary to it. Therefore men of knowledge must fail. The plan must still be carried on by men of faith, until the final revelation of the Lord ; of His kingdom Israel ; and of His true church ; shall make the whole plan a matter of knowledge to all the world.

Therefore we, having put our hand to the great task, will " carry on," doing our bit in this the one great work of all the ages.

" Now the just shall live by faith, but if any man draw back, my soul shall have no pleasure in him."

" But we are not of them which draw back unto perdition ; but of them that believe to the saving of the soul." (Heb. x, 38, 39.)

With the fathers the whole plan was a matter of faith, for with them it was only beginning. With us it is already very largely become a matter of knowledge, and every additional item of knowledge of the out-working of the great plan makes faith easier, and more unavoidable. To this end there is given a very wonderful synopsis of the progress of the plan through the ages in the eleventh and twelfth chapters of this great Epistle, as there is a still more wonderful history of that progress in the historical books of the Bible. To the synopsis of that progress we will now give attention, taking note that every person and every event named are outstanding either in the life of the covenant-bearing fathers before Abraham, or

in the Abraham-Israel line from the call of
Abraham.

Since the writing of that wonderful Epistle of
the Hebrews, the history of Israel in the Celto-
Saxon nation and company of nations has been
just as steadily progressing. A new chapter of
Hebrews has been written in the histories of
Anglo-Saxondom in that book which Isaiah names
as " the book of Jehovah." That is to say, in the
book of world history pivoting as it does on
Israel Britain. For while man writes history,
God makes it. And all history is an added part
of the Bible. The Bible gives prophecy to cover
all the ages, and history furnishes the fulfilment.

Let us turn to the demonstration of the wonderful progress of the great plan as epitomised in
the xi and xii Hebrews.

The following is the Divine age-long demonstration of the facts which form the basis of our
faith :

" Now faith is the substance of things hoped
for, the evidence of things not seen.

For by it the elders obtained a good report.

Through faith we understand that the worlds
were framed by the word of God.

By faith Abel offered a more excellent sacrifice . . .

By faith Enoch was translated . . . (thus
becoming the first fruits of the translation, even
as Jesus Christ is the first fruit from the dead).

By faith Noah, being warned by God of things
not seen as yet, moved with fear, prepared an ark,
to the saving of his house . . .

By faith Abraham, when he was called to go out into a place which he should after receive for an inheritance, obeyed; and he went out not knowing whither he went . . .

By faith he sojourned in the land of promise, as in a strange country; dwelling in tabernacles, with Isaac and Jacob, the heirs with him of the same promise:

FOR HE LOOKED FOR A CITY
WHICH HATH FOUNDATIONS
WHOSE BUILDER AND MAKER IS GOD.

Through faith also Sarah herself received strength to CONCEIVE SEED, and was delivered of a child when she was past age, because she judged HIM FAITHFUL WHO HAD PROMISED.

THEREFORE sprang there even of one, and him as good as dead, so many as the stars of the sky in multitude, and as the sand which is by the seashore innumerable.

These all DIED IN FAITH, not having received the promises, but having seen them afar off,

And were persuaded of them,

And embraced them,

And confessed that they were strangers and pilgrims on the earth.

For they that say such things declare plainly that they SEEK A COUNTRY. . . . God is not ashamed to be called their God; FOR HE HATH PREPARED FOR THEM A CITY.

These all died in the faith, not having received the promises."

Thus are the pre-Abraham worthies presented to us.

" By faith Abraham when he was tried OFFERED UP ISAAC ; and he that had received the promises offered up his only begotten son, of whom it was said, THAT IN ISAAC SHALL THY SEED BE CALLED.

Accounting that God was able to raise him up even from the dead ; from whence also he received him in a figure.

By faith Isaac blessed Jacob and Esau concerning things to come.

By faith Jacob, when he was a dying, blessed both the sons of Joseph (thus starting great prophetic events which have governed the course of history to this day).

By faith Joseph, when he died, made mention of the departing of the children of Israel ; and gave commandment concerning his bones.

By faith Moses when he was born, was hid three months of his parents.

By faith Moses when he was come to years, REFUSED TO BE CALLED THE SON OF PHARAOH'S DAUGHTER ;

Choosing rather to suffer affliction with the people of God, than to enjoy the pleasures of sin for a season ;

ESTEEMING THE REPROACH OF CHRIST greater riches than the treasures of Egypt ; for he had respect unto the recompense of the reward.

By faith he forsook Egypt, not fearing the wrath of the King ; for he ENDURED AS SEEING HIM WHO IS INVISIBLE.

Through faith he kept the passover,
And the sprinkling of blood . . .
By faith they passed through the Red Sea as
on dry ground . . .
By faith the walls of Jericho fell down . . .
By faith the harlot Rahab perished not . . .
And what shall I more say ? for the time would
fail me to tell of

Gidean,
Barak,
Samson,
Jephthae,
David,
Samuel,
And of the prophets.
Who through faith
Subdued kingdoms,
Wrought righteousness,
Obtained promises,
Stopped the mouths of lions,
Quenched the violence of fire,
Escaped the edge of the sword,
Out of weakness were made strong,
Waxed valiant in fight,
Turned to flight the armies of the aliens.
Women received their dead raised to life
    again.

Mileposts along the route of Israel's march down the ages.

And others were tortured not accepting deliver-
ance ; THAT THEY MIGHT OBTAIN A BETTER
RESURRECTION :

THE STATESMANSHIP OF JESUS

(Heb. xi, 36-40.)

36. " And others had trial of *cruel* mockings and scourgings, yea, moreover of bonds and imprisonment :

37. They were stoned, they were sawn asunder, were tempted, were slain with the sword ; they wandered about in sheepskins and goatskins ; being destitute, afflicted, tormented ;

38. (Of whom the world was not worthy :) they wandered in deserts, and *in* mountains, and *in* dens and caves of the earth.

39. And these all, having obtained a good report through faith, received not the promise :

40. God having provided some better thing for us, that they without us should not be made perfect."

Here we have manifested before us a list of historic persons, and of historic events, and every such person and event from Abel to Noah, from Noah to Abraham, and *so directly down is the line of Seth*, Shem, of Israel prophecy and history.

The whole scheme of fact and truth follows the great highway of Israel prophecy, along which have tramped the hosts of the generations in succession ; each in turn helping along the transformation of *Israel-prophecy* into *world history* of the most vital kind.

Each generation took up the march where the faltering steps of the preceding generation halted, and carried the banner of the Covenant (the Brith), forward for the stage appointed to it.

The dying hands of the one passed the standard to the youthful hands of the succeeding standard-bearing generation.

Each generation in turn has followed the standard as far as the distance allotted to its short life has permitted, and each generation will do so to the end. It is the relay march of Israel-Britain, the Sons of God through the ages, toward the Millennial glory of the Kingdom.

From united Israel, the Standard went for a time to the House of Judah when the ten tribes revolted.

When in turn the House of Judah rejected the Christ, He declared "The Kingdom is taken from you and given to a nation bringing forth the fruits thereof."

Isaiah and Jeremiah, etc., inform us that thereafter it returned to Israel in the Isles, including the ten tribes.

That nation, the Celto-Saxon people, grasped the Standard, and has been carrying it forward to the ends of the earth as it is to-day.

Again, the Standard will be handed to our coming Lord, when He shall return to reign in Zion, upon the throne of David, over the House of Jacob, for ever.

The great racial march is still in progress. The tramping of millions of feet in the unhalting march still echoes in the courts of heaven. Where is the end of the march?

The end is at the city which God has promised and prepared. This was the goal of Abraham,

Isaac and Jacob, and it is still the goal of the people of God.

When and where shall we come to that city?

This is clearly shown in the last chapters of the Bible, in the post-Millennial glory.

To this great goal the Lord our Saviour will lead the marching hosts of Israel during the last millennium of earth history. The ranks of the marching armies are even now awaiting the coming of our Lord. The cry has gone forth, " Behold the bridegroom cometh ; go ye out to meet Him."

" Wherefore seeing we also are compassed about with so great a cloud of witnesses, let us lay aside every weight ; and the sin which doth so easily beset us, and let us run with patience the RACE WHICH IS SET BEFORE US.

Looking unto Jesus, the author and finisher of our faith.

Who for the joy that was set before him, ENDURED THE CROSS, DESPISING THE SHAME, and is set down at the right hand of the throne of God.

For consider him that endured such contradiction of sinners against himself, lest ye be wearied and faint in your minds.

Ye have not yet resisted unto blood striving against sin."

Yes, Jesus is the author of your faith. He is the Originator of the plan. He is the Giver of the promises.

He is the constant Leader of the generations as each in turn takes up the march.

He is the Redeemer of Israel, and the Saviour of men.

He is the King that is coming to take up the Kingship in Israel, during the last millennium of the march. He is " the author and the finisher of our faith."

And now let us look for a moment at the first statement. " Now faith is the substance of things hoped for, the evidence of things not seen."

What are the things hoped for ?

They are " A country " and " A city " in which the massed generations of Israel shall dwell for ever.

For nearly four thousand years they have been carrying on the great relay march through the ages, marching in column according to the plan of march set forth in the first chapters of Numbers. But now the long, long march is nearly finished, and the permanent camp is to be formed which shall continue during the millennial reign of our Lord. The order of the camp is also given in the same chapters of Numbers.

Of the verity of all this we have as " evidence," the " substance " of the kingdom which has been assembled before our eyes in the seed of Israel in all their generations ; in the lands given of the fathers ; in the history of the nations of Israel in their various divisions to this day ; in the first coming of our Lord ; in the history of the Christian Church ; IN THE HISTORY OF THE CELTO-SAXON peoples down to this day ; in the present state of world affairs ; and in the evident signs which mark the coming of the Son of Man to reign ;

such indisputable "evidence" are the facts of history, which present the accumulated "substance" of the plan now nearing completion.

Many years ago, the writer landed in the Dominion of Canada. There were then about five millions of a population only. The people were talking excitedly of undertaking to build a trans-continental railway from the Atlantic to the Pacific—the first to be built across the continent of North America. They were fighting a political election on the question "to build or not to build." One party pledged itself that the road should be built ; the other party declared it could not be built by such a handful of people ; if it were, " it would not pay for the axle grease of the rolling stock, and would be a financial disaster."

It looked as though the latter were right ; there were 3,000 miles of wilderness to be crossed, including 1,000 miles of the savage rock region between Ontario and Winnipeg, and 800 miles of tremendous mountain engineering from Calgary to Vancouver. So the people did not believe the railroad would be built. By and by there appeared enormous quantities of material for railroad construction ; timber for bridges ; timber for stations ; timber for the roadbed ; steel rails in great quantities ; engines and carriages, etc., the substance out of which a railroad is constructed.

The substance so brought and placed became the evidence that in very deed the road was to be constructed.

With this evidence before their eyes, the faith

of the people developed. Now what had happened?

A group of courageous men invested their capital and borrowed to the limit of their credit, in order *to produce the material substance* which should become *the evidence*, out of which should arise *the faith* of the investing public. The faith, as developed, resulted in the production of the money, and the road was built.

Thus the substance became the evidence, and the evidence became the faith of the people. In like manner the substance of the kingdom becomes the evidence of the kingdom, and the evidence becomes the faith of the Kingdom, and faith is the substance of things hoped for and the evidence of things not seen.

What is the substance which becomes the evidence in this case ?

1. The LORD who is faithful. He is at the base of all faith.

2. Then the land promised to the fathers, " the appointed place " (II Sam. vii), then added " the heathen for an inheritance," and " the uttermost parts of the earth for a possession."

3. The covenants made with the fathers.

4. The race developed through the fathers.

5. The prophecy given through the fathers in the Old Testament, and through the Son in the New Testament.

6. The history enacted by the fathers in the B.C. generations, and by their British-Israel descendants in the A.D. generations down to the present day.

All these facts combined assure us the sacrifices of the fathers and of the present generation of all that is attractive in the present life, in order that we may follow the beaten path of the generations of Israel, will be rewarded by the ultimate finding of the COUNTRY and of the CITY which our race has been ever seeking and ever waiting for since Abraham first . . . went out not knowing whither he went.

" Wherefore God is not ashamed to be called their God, FOR HE HATH PREPARED FOR THEM A CITY."

The country will be found by them renewed by the creative act of God to be possessed by them for ever. The city will eventually appear as is so clearly made manifest in the last two chapters of Revelation.

For the guidance of our conduct in the march let us read carefully the general instructions issued from the Lord—in the succeeding paragraphs of the great Epistle.

(Heb. xiii, 20-21.)

20. " Now the God of peace, that brought again from the dead our Lord Jesus, that great Shepherd of the sheep, through the blood of the everlasting covenant,

21. Make you perfect in every good work to do his will, working in you that which is well-pleasing in his sight, through Jesus Christ ; to whom be glory for ever and ever. Amen."

CHAPTER XII

THE GOAL

LET us consider the goal toward which ourselves, our nation, our race are travelling.

" They seek a city, which hath foundations ; whose builder and maker is God."

The CITY is the goal of the hopes of the children of Abraham, Isaac and Jacob, to which seed by the grace of God we belong.

In seeking the City they have expected (and we still expect), to spend their lives, their efforts, and their treasure.

In seeking the City, they have determined to refuse all other attractions of whatever nature which would lure from the quest. This is true of the greatest things of the earth.

Abraham might have remained in Ur of the Chaldees ; and we may take it for granted that his position would not have been an humble one there.

Moses was called the Son of Pharaoh's daughter, and as such would have succeeded to the throne and the " treasures of Egypt," but because he sought the City, he refused to be called the son of Pharaoh's daughter.

Because he sought the City he went forth from Egypt, " not fearing the wrath of the King," but fearing to be turned aside from the quest of the

City, and from his share of the great march of Israel through the ages in the quest of it.

Jesus was offered " all the kingdoms of the world and the glory of them," but he " refused the evil and chose the good," even though the way of the " good " was the way of the cross.

The generations of worthies recorded in the eleventh chapter of the Epistle of the Hebrews refused the attractions of life by the wayside, "choosing rather to suffer affliction with the people of God, than to enjoy the pleasures of sin for a season."

What is the City these sought ?

God is preparing the final City in the heavens, which shall in due time be revealed.

In the meantime He has given to us the privilege of reproducing the City on the earth, according to our ideals and plans.

Accordingly, while the mystical City is in progress of preparation for the day of final triumphant revelation, the City has in the meantime an earthly manifestation. The record of this stands out most clearly in the Bible.

That the Kingdoms of this world have emulated and surpassed the earthly manifestation in splendour is a great fact of history which we have not time to deal with here.

The City has a double significance, fitting in perfectly to the Great plan. It is at once

Jerusalem   -   -   and   -   -   Zion.

It emerges first upon the pages of history as Salem. That majestic and mysterious personage who came to Abraham and blessed him, as the greater blesses the lesser—Melchisedec—was King of Salem.

During Joshua's time the King of Salem was Adonizedek. The former was King of Peace, and the latter Lord of Peace.

David captured the City, enlarged and beautified it, and called it Zion, instituting the Zion administration which should endure forever. There he " sat upon the throne of Jehovah as king," as did Solomon his son and successor. (I Chron. xxix, 23.)

Solomon built therein the Temple, and made it the centre of worship for the world, under the name of Jerusalem.

Zion the centre of Government, and Jerusalem the centre of worship, both of Jehovah.

Of *Zion* we have this wonderful description in the forty-eighth Psalm, which sets forth the Kingship of Jehovah established there.

The Kingly administration. Psalm xlviii.

1. " Great is the Lord, and greatly to be praised in the city of our God, in the mountain of his holiness.

2. Beautiful for situation, the joy of the whole earth, is mount Zion, on the sides of the north, the city of the great King.

3. God is known in her palaces for a refuge.

4. For, lo, the kings were assembled, they passed by together.

5. They saw it, and so they marvelled ; they were troubled, and hasted away.

6. Fear took hold upon them there, and pain, as of a woman in travail.

7. Thou breakest the ships of Tarshish with an east wind.

8. As we have heard, so have we seen in the city of the Lord of hosts, in the city of our God : God will establish it for ever. Selah."

The glory of the temple worship.

9. " We have thought of thy lovingkindness, O God, in the midst of thy temple.

10. According to thy name, O God, so is thy praise unto the ends of the earth : thy right hand is full of righteousness."

The defences of Zion.

11. " Let mount Zion rejoice, let the daughters of Judah be glad, because of thy judgments.

12. Walk about Zion, and go round about her : tell the towers thereof.

13. Mark ye well her bulwarks, consider her palaces ; that ye may tell it to the generation following.

14. For this God is our God for ever and ever : he will be our guide even unto death."

Of the City Isaiah speaks in chapter lii thus :

The ultimate glory. Isaiah lii, 1-3, 7-8.

1. " Awake, awake ; put on thy strength, O Zion ; put on thy beautiful garments, O Jerusalem, the holy city : for henceforth there shall no more come into thee the uncircumcised and the unclean.

2. Shake thyself from the dust ; arise, and sit down, O Jerusalem : loose thyself from the bands of thy neck, O captive daughter of Zion.

3. For thus saith the Lord, Ye have sold yourselves for nought ; and ye shall be redeemed without money.

7. How beautiful upon the mountains are the feet of him that bringeth good tidings, that publisheth peace ; that bringeth good tidings of good, that publisheth salvation ; that saith unto Zion, Thy God reigneth!

8. Thy watchmen shall lift up the voice ; with the voice together shall they sing : for they shall see eye to eye, when the Lord shall bring again Zion.

9. Break forth into joy, sing together, ye waste places of Jerusalem : for the Lord hath comforted his people, he hath redeemed Jerusalem.

10. The Lord hath made bare his holy arm in the eyes of all the nations ; and all the ends of the earth shall see the salvation of our God."

Jehovah hath set His name for ever in the City.

God has set His King on the Holy Hill of Zion.

" Yet have I set my King on my holy hill of Zion.

I will declare the decree : the LORD hath said unto me, Thou art my Son ; this day have I begotten thee.

Ask of me and I shall give to thee the heathen for thine inheritance, and the uttermost parts of the earth for thy possession."

During the continuance of the Kingdom in

Zion, belonging to no one of the tribes separately, but to all of the tribes collectively, the City was the capital of the Kingdom of the House of David until the Kingdom was removed in the days of Zedekiah.

Jesus came to the city with ceremonial, fulfilling the prophecies ; and there He was cast out of the city and crucified.

Thus He suffered outside of the city which was officially the " Camp " of the Hosts of God.

THE KINGDOM REMOVED.

Jesus said to the inhabitants of the city : " Behold the Kingdom is taken from you and given to a nation bringing forth the fruits thereof."

Of the city he said (Matt. xxiii, 37-39) :

37. " O Jerusalem, Jerusalem, thou that killest the prophets, and stonest them which are sent unto thee, how often would I have gathered thy children together, even as a hen gathereth her chickens under her wings, and ye would not !

38. Behold, your house is left unto you desolate.

39. For I say unto you, Ye shall not see me henceforth, till ye shall say, Blessed is he that cometh in the name of the Lord."

Whence did the Kingdom go ?

It went to a nation; for this the Lord distinctly assures us.

It could only go to an Israel nation. It was to Israel that the Lord said " Ye shall be a peculiar treasure above all people, for all the earth is mine.

And ye shall be unto me a Kingdom of priests; and an holy nation."

All the Scriptures which deal with this great theme of the Kingdom bear out clearly the fact that only an Israel nation could receive the Kingdom.

There has always been in existence an Israel nation to receive the Kingdom, as the New Covenant here quoted shows:

(Jer. xxxi and Heb. viii.)

31. " Behold, the days come, saith the Lord, that I will make a new covenant with the house of Israel, and with the house of Judah:

32. Not according to the covenant that I made with their fathers in the day that I took them by the hand to bring them out of the land of Egypt; which my covenant they brake, although I was an husband unto them, saith the Lord:

33. But this shall be the covenant that I will make with the house of Israel; After those days, saith the Lord, I will put my law in their inward parts, and write it in their hearts; and will be their God, and they shall be my people.

34. And they shall teach no more every man his neighbour, and every man his brother, saying, Know the Lord: for they shall all know me, from the least of them unto the greatest of them, saith the Lord: for I will forgive their iniquity, and I will remember their sin no more."

7. " For if that first covenant had been faultless, then should no place have been sought for the second.

8. For finding fault with them, he saith, Behold, the days come, saith the Lord, when I will make a new covenant with the house of Israel and with the house of Judah :

9. Not according to the covenant that I made with their fathers in the day when I took them by the hand to lead them out of the land of Egypt ; because they continued not in my covenant, and I regarded them not, saith the Lord.

10. For this is the covenant that I will make with the house of Israel after those days, saith the Lord ; I will put my laws into their mind, and write them in their hearts : and I will be to them a God, and they shall be to me a people :

11. And they shall not teach every man his neighbour, and every man his brother, saying, Know the Lord : for all shall know me, from the least to the greatest.

12. For I will be merciful to their unrighteousness, and their sins and their iniquities will I remember no more.

13. In that he saith, A new covenant, he hath made the first old. Now that which decayeth and waxeth old is ready to vanish away."

The plain statement of the renewal of the Covenant with the House of David at the time that it was being removed from Jerusalem is that " David shall never want a man to sit upon the throne of the House of Israel," as the following renewal of the Covenant with the House of David shows.

THE GOAL

(Jer. xxxiii.)

1. "Moreover the word of the Lord came unto Jeremiah the second time, while he was yet shut up in the court of the prison, saying,

2. Thus saith the Lord the maker thereof, the Lord that formed it, to establish it, the Lord is his name ;

3. Call unto me, and I will answer thee, and shew thee great and mighty things, which thou knowest not.

4. For thus saith the Lord, the God of Israel, concerning the houses of this city, and concerning the houses of the kings of Judah, which are thrown down by the mounts, and by the sword ;

5. They come to fight with the Chaldeans, but it is to fill them with the dead bodies of men, whom I have slain in mine anger and in my fury, and for all whose wickedness I have hid my face from this city.

6. Behold, I will bring it health and cure, and I will cure them, and will reveal unto them the abundance of peace and truth.

7. And I will cause the captivity of Judah and the captivity of Israel to return, and will build them, as at the first.

8. And I will cleanse them from all their iniquity, whereby they have sinned against me : and I will pardon all their iniquities, whereby they have sinned, and whereby they have transgressed against me.

9. And it shall be to me a name of joy, a praise and an honour before all the nations of the earth,

which shall hear all the good that I do unto them : and they shall fear and tremble for all the goodness and for all the prosperity that I procure unto it.

10. Thus saith the Lord ; Again there shall be heard in this place, which ye say shall be desolate without man and without beast, even in the cities of Judah, and in the streets of Jerusalem, that are desolate, without man, and without inhabitant, and without beast,

11. The voice of joy, and the voice of gladness, the voice of the bridegroom, and the voice of the bride, the voice of them that shall say, praise the Lord of hosts : for the Lord is good ; for his mercy endureth for ever : and of them that shall bring the sacrifice of praise into the house of the Lord. For I will cause to return the captivity of the land, as at the first, saith the Lord.

12. Thus saith the Lord of hosts ; Again in this place, which is desolate without man and without beast, and in all the cities thereof, shall be an habitation of shepherds causing their flocks to lie down.

13. In the cities of the mountains, in the cities of the vale, and in the cities of the south, and in the land of Benjamin, and in the places about Jerusalem, and in the cities of Judah, shall the flocks pass again under the hands of him that telleth them, saith the Lord.

14. Behold, the days come, saith the Lord, that I will perform the good thing which I have promised unto the house of Israel and to the house of Judah.

15. In those days, and at that time, will I cause the Branch of righteousness to grow up unto David; and he shall execute judgment and righteousness in the land.

16. In those days shall Judah be saved, and Jerusalem shall dwell safely: and this is the name wherewith she shall be called, The Lord our righteousness.

17. For thus saith the Lord; David shall never want a man to sit upon the throne of the house of Israel;

18. Neither shall the priests the Levites want a man before me to offer burnt offerings, and to kindle meat offerings, and to do sacrifice continually.

19. And the word of the Lord came unto Jeremiah, saying,

20. Thus saith the Lord; If ye can break my covenant of the day, and my covenant of the night, and that there should not be day and night in their season;

21. Then may also my covenant be broken with David my servant, that he should not have a son to reign upon his throne; and with the Levites the priests, my ministers.

22. As the hosts of heaven cannot be numbered, neither the sand of the sea measured; so will I multiply the seed of David my servant, and the Levites that minister unto me.

23. Moreover the word of the Lord came to Jeremiah, saying,

24. Considerest thou not what this people have

spoken, saying, The two families which the Lord hath chosen, he hath even cast them off ? thus they have despised my people, and they should be no more a nation before them.

25. Thus saith the Lord ; If my covenant be not with day and night, and if I have not appointed the ordinances of heaven and earth ;

26. Then will I cast away the seed of Jacob, and David my servant, so that I will not take any of his seed to be rulers over the seed of Abraham, Isaac, and Jacob : for I will cause their captivity to return, and have mercy on them."

Writing concerning the Official City, Zechariah declares : " Jerusalem shall be *inhabited again in its own place even in Jerusalem*," and Isaiah says of Zion, " My watchmen shall see eye to eye when I BRING AGAIN Zion."

We therefore see that both official Zion and Jerusalem have been absent from geographical Jerusalem since the time of the removal of the Kingdom.

We see further that Isaiah in his great Israel in the Isles message, which begins with the fortieth chapter, addresses both Jerusalem and Zion as being in the Isles.

We must therefore look for these national centres as being in the Isles where Israel should dwell during the present dispensation. This is so manifestly the case that we believe there is not the slightest reason to doubt or to question the matter.

Already there is a promise of the return of

official Zion to geographical Zion in the fact that once more Jerusalem has extended its power to Jerusalem geographical (that is to say, the Government has extended its power to the ancient city of the fathers) and has there established a branch of its Government once more.

Thus the promise of the New Covenant concerning the City contained in Jeremiah xxxi is in process of fulfilment.

Official Jerusalem, the centre of the national worship, has also a thriving Bishopric in Jerusalem, but the government will not be allowed to go unchallenged. The City will again be besieged by alien power and will be taken. " The houses shall be rifled and the women ravished and half of the city shall go into captivity."

" In that day His feet shall stand upon the Mount of Olives," and the Lord will return to the City, and the City will be permanently regained.

THE MILLENNIAL CITY.

Then will come the building of the new City to serve during the Millennial reign of our Lord, and of the new Temple to be the centre of His worship.

" The City lieth four square," " And the suburbs of the City shall be TOWARD THE NORTH two hundred and fifty, and TOWARD THE SOUTH two hundred and fifty, and TOWARD THE EAST two hundred and fifty, and TOWARD THE WEST two hundred and fifty."

For the full description of the Temple, the City,

and the land as it shall be divided among the tribes see Ezekiel, chapters xlii to xlviii.

To this land shall return the tribes of Israel, as is geographically set forth in Ezekiel xxxvi, 1-15.

To this City shall return the Glory of God, which departed from the former City of Jerusalem, and which accompanied Israel in its wanderings and abode with her in the appointed place.

.   .   .   .

This is the earthly city. But in the meantime this is but the temporary city which has been set up first in Palestine, then in Israel in the Isles in the land and nation of Israel.

The description of the final city is as follows :

AND I SAW THE HOLY CITY,

New Jerusalem coming down from God out of heaven prepared as a bride adorned for her husband.

(Rev. xxi, 3-4.)

" And I heard a great voice out of heaven saying, Behold, the tabernacle of God is with men, and he will dwell with them, and they shall be his people, and God himself shall be with them, and be their God.

And God shall wipe away all tears from their eyes ; and there shall be no more death, neither sorrow, nor crying, neither shall there be any more pain : for the former things are passed away."

(Rev. xxi, 10-27.)

10. " And he carried me away in the spirit to a great and high mountain, and showed me that great city, the holy Jerusalem, descending out of heaven from God :

11. Having the glory of God : and her light was like unto a stone most precious, even like a jasper stone, clear as crystal ;

12. And had a wall great and high, and had twelve gates, and at the gates twelve angels, and names written thereon, which are the names of the twelve tribes of the children of Israel :

13. On the east, three gates ; on the north, three gates ; on the south, three gates ; and on the west, three gates.

14. And the wall of the city had twelve foundations, and in them the names of the twelve apostles of the Lamb.

15. And he that talked with me had a golden reed to measure the city, and the gates thereof, and the wall thereof.

16. And the city lieth four-square, and the length is as large as the breadth. And he measured the city with the reed, twelve thousand furlongs. The length, and the breadth, and the height of it are equal.

17. And he measured the wall thereof, an hundred and forty and four cubits, according to the measure of a man, that is, of the angel.

18. And the building of the wall was of jasper: and the city was pure gold, like unto clear glass.

19. And the foundations of the wall of the city

were garnished with all manner of precious stones. The first foundation was jasper ; the second, sapphire ; the third, a chalcedony ; the fourth, an emerald ;

20. The fifth, sardonyx ; the sixth, sardius ; the seventh, chrysolite ; the eighth, beryl ; the ninth, a topaz ; the tenth, a chrysoprasus ; the eleventh, a jacinth ; the twelfth, an amethyst.

21. And the twelve gates were twelve pearls ; every several gate was of one pearl : and the street of the city was pure gold, as it were transparent glass.

22. And I saw no temple therein : for the Lord God Almighty and the Lamb are the temple of it.

23. And the city had no need of the sun, neither of the moon, to shine in it ; for the glory of God did lighten it, and the Lamb is the light thereof.

24. And the nations of them which are saved shall walk in the light of it : and the kings of the earth do bring their glory and honour into it.

25. And the gates of it shall not be shut at all by day : for there shall be no night there.

26. And they shall bring the glory and honour of the nations into it.

27. And there shall in no wise enter into it any thing that defileth, neither whatsoever workest abomination or maketh a lie ; but they which are written in the Lamb's book of life."

" They seek for a city which hath foundations, Whose builder and maker is God." This is the goal of the march through the ages of the Israel people.

CHAPTER XIII

The Country

But also it is written from the beginning, " They seek a country."

" For they that say such things declare plainly that they seek a country."

And truly, if they had been mindful of that country from whence they came out, they might have had opportunity to have returned.

But now they desire a better country, that is, an heavenly : wherefore God is not ashamed to be called their God : for He hath prepared for them a city.

The description of the country which they sought and we, their successors, still seek, will be found in Rev. xxii, 1-6, as follows :

1. " And he showed me a pure river of water of life, clear as crystal, proceeding out of the throne of God and of the Lamb.

2. In the midst of the street of it, and on either side of the river, was there the tree of life, which bare twelve manner of fruits, and yielded her fruit every month : and the leaves of the tree were for the healing of the nations.

3. And there shall be no more curse ; but the throne of God and of the Lamb shall be in it ; and his servants shall serve him :

4. And they shall see his face ; and his name shall be in their foreheads.

5. And there shall be no night there; and they need no candle, neither light of the sun ; for the Lord God giveth them light : and they shall reign for ever and ever.

6. And he said unto me, These sayings are faithful and true : and the Lord God of the holy prophets sent his angel to show unto his servants the things which must shortly be done.

The invitation to become citizens of that country is contained in the following sentences :
" And the Spirit and the bride say, Come.
" And let him that heareth say, Come.
" And let him that is athirst come.
" And whosoever will, let him take of the water of life freely."

THE END